"Howard Baker's *The One True Thing* will help you seek, choose, and value God above all else and hence to more deeply experience life eternal and abundant in Christ."

— REV. SIANG-YANG TAN, Ph.D., professor of psychology, Fuller Theological Seminary; senior pastor, First Evangelical Church, Glendale, California

"Do you long to transform your struggling spirit into a peaceful source of love and strength? Howard's book both challenged and quieted my spirit as he called me to rediscover the job of being Christ's disciple."

— CRAIG WILLIFORD, Ph.D., president, Denver Seminary

What Is Worthy of Your

Lifelong Devotion?

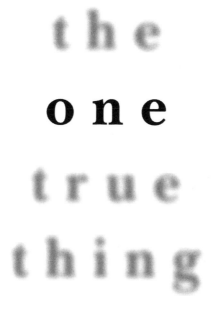

the
one
true
thing

HOWARD BAKER

NAVPRESS®

BRINGING TRUTH TO LIFE

OUR GUARANTEE TO YOU

We believe so strongly in the message of our books that we are making this quality guarantee to you. If for any reason you are disappointed with the content of this book, return the title page to us with your name and address and we will refund to you the list price of the book. To help us serve you better, please briefly describe why you were disappointed. Mail your refund request to: NavPress, P.O. Box 35002, Colorado Springs, CO 80935.

The Navigators is an international Christian organization. Our mission is to advance the gospel of Jesus and His kingdom into the nations through spiritual generations of laborers living and discipling among the lost. We see a vital movement of the gospel, fueled by prevailing prayer, flowing freely through relational networks and out into the nations where workers for the kingdom are next door to everywhere.

NavPress is the publishing ministry of The Navigators. The mission of NavPress is to reach, disciple, and equip people to know Christ and make Him known by publishing life-related materials that are biblically rooted and culturally relevant. Our vision is to stimulate spiritual transformation through every product we publish.

ISBN-13: 978-1-57683-695-8
ISBN-10: 1-57683-695-9

Cover design by Arvid Wallen
Creative Team: Don Simpson, Reagen Reed, Arvid Wallen, Kathy Guist

Some of the anecdotal illustrations in this book are true to life and are included with the permission of the persons involved. All other illustrations are composites of real situations, and any resemblance to people living or dead is coincidental.

Unless otherwise identified, all Scripture quotations in this publication are taken from the *New American Standard Bible* (NASB), © The Lockman Foundation 1960, 1962, 1963, 1968, 1971, 1972, 1973, 1975, 1977, 1995. The author's paraphrases and translations are marked as PAR. Other versions used include: the HOLY BIBLE: NEW INTERNATIONAL VERSION® (NIV®). Copyright © 1973, 1978, 1984 by International Bible Society. Used by permission of Zondervan Publishing House. All rights reserved; *THE MESSAGE* (MSG). Copyright © 1993, 1994, 1995, 1996, 2000, 2001, 2002, 2005. Used by permission of NavPress Publishing Group; the *Revised Standard Version Bible* (RSV), copyright 1946, 1952, 1971, by the Division of Christian Education of the National Council of the Churches of Christ in the USA, used by permission, all rights reserved; the *New Revised Standard Version* (NRSV), copyright © 1989, by the Division of Christian Education of the National Council of the Churches of Christ in the USA, used by permission, all rights reserved; the *New King James Version* (NKJV). Copyright © 1982 by Thomas Nelson, Inc. Used by permission. All rights reserved; and the *English Standard Version* (ESV), copyright © 2001 by Crossway Bibles, a division of Good News Publishers. Used by permission. All rights reserved.

Baker, Howard, 1951-
  The one true thing : what is worthy of your lifelong devotion? / Howard Baker.
    p. cm.
  Includes bibliographical references.
  ISBN 1-57683-695-9
  1. Spiritual life--Christianity. I. Title.
BV4501.3.B354 2007
248.4--dc22
                        2006031471

Printed in the United States of America

1 2 3 4 5 6 7 8 / 11 10 09 08 07

FOR A FREE CATALOG OF NAVPRESS BOOKS & BIBLE STUDIES,
CALL 1-800-366-7788 (USA) OR 1-800-839-4769 (CANADA)

For
Cody and Keely

There are many who have the fading delight of being an author,
But I alone have the lasting joy of being your dad.

What is writ small on the pages of this book about
The One True Thing
Is writ large on the pages of your lives.

You are evidence that lives are more reliable witnesses
to Jesus than books.

Deep in the heart of [every person] is the longing, fitfully glimpsed and but half realized, to gather up all [its] strivings into an intense pursuit of one all-embracing objective worthy of the toil and tears and devotion of the human heart.

— KARL RAHNER

Contents

Preface   11

Introduction: The Only True Thing   15

PART 1: Seeking the One Thing — A Pure and Holy Passion

1. Psalm 27: Seeking the One Thing over the Many   25
2. Julian of Norwich: The Life of Seeking the One Thing   35
3. Jesus' Invitation to Seek the One Thing   45

PART 2: Choosing the One Thing — A Magnificent Obsession

4. Luke 10:38-42: Choosing the One Thing over the Many   57
5. Søren Kierkegaard: The Life of Choosing the One Thing   65
6. Jesus' Invitation to Choose the One Thing   75

PART 3: Valuing the One Thing — A Glorious Ambition

7. Philippians 3: Valuing the One Thing over the Many   89
8. Ignatius of Loyola: The Life of Valuing the One Thing   97
9. Jesus' Invitation to Value the One Thing   107

Afterword   117

Notes   121

About the Author   133

Preface

My journey into the One Thing has been bracketed by the same Doctor of Ministry class, taken once for credit and once as an audit student. The first time was in 1990 and was taught by Eugene Peterson. The replay was in 2005 and was taught by Dallas Willard. Over the course of those intervening fifteen years, the spoken and written words of these two contemporary spiritual guides have so permeated my heart and mind that I can scarcely say or write anything about relationship with Jesus that was not planted in me by them. I pray what I write (and live) is as faithful to the written and Living Word as what they taught me. Where it is not, I claim full responsibility. Where it is, I owe to Dallas and Eugene an immeasurable debt of gratitude.

In an interview, author Donald Miller said that his local congregation in Portland, Oregon — called Imago Dei — makes him feel parented and connected. He tells the story about speaking at his church when a woman, a homosexual, was sitting in the front row with a giant sign that said (among other things) that she hoped the churchgoers' children die and the legacy of hate ends.

He finishes the story, "At the end of the service, her sign was laid down in front of the communion table, and she was being held by me, and many others, sobbing as she had never heard truth being presented in love. She had not known the difference between a parental communication of truth and a judgmental, hate-filled communication of truth."[1]

My prayer is that anyone who reads this book will have an

experience of being held in the arms of a loving community—Father, Son, and Holy Spirit, along with the great cloud of witnesses who have asked for, chosen, and valued the one true thing. I pray that the words will be not only true, but true to the God who is love—making them loving words as well as true words.

During the writing of this book, I was using *Introduction to the Devout Life* by Francis de Sales for a seminary class I was teaching. His words express my heart in writing a book such as this:

> It is true, my dear reader that I write about the devout life although I myself am not devout. Yet it is certainly not without a desire of becoming so and it is such affection that encourages me to instruct you. As a great man of letters has said, "To study is a good way to learn; to hear is a still better way; to teach is the best of all."[2]

Several students from that class were also in my Spiritual Direction Practicum. Their discernment, prayer, and encouragement kept this project moving in spite of the opposition of the evil one, my own sinful procrastination, and the challenge of writing in the midst of an already-full workload. Thank you, Julie, Louise, Mark, and Shira.

Don Simpson, the skilled editor of this book, is just as much a saint as any that I quote or write about. I simply bless God for reflecting the glory of the face of Christ through Don's patience, graciousness, humility, and faithfulness in the midst of physical and emotional affliction. Because Don experiences the one true thing in the depths of his soul, he wanted me to write about it. He was, and is, more qualified to write about it than I am. Thank you, Don, for giving me the opportunity and for not letting me give up.

Jesus said that "out of the overflow of the heart the mouth speaks" (Matthew 12:34, NIV), and, I would add, the hand writes.

The one my heart loves is also the one God has most used to shape that heart. Thank you, Janis, for loving me out of the "many things" so I was free to embrace the one thing necessary.

Introduction

The Only True Thing

And this is the real and eternal life:
That they know you,
The one and only true God,
And Jesus Christ, whom you sent.
— JOHN 17:3 (MSG)

Our true life is not this external, material life that passes before our
eyes here on earth, but the inner life of our spirit, for which the visible
life serves only as a scaffolding — a necessary aid to our
spiritual growth.
— LEO TOLSTOY

The one thing God keeps us to steadily is that
we may be one with Jesus Christ.
— OSWALD CHAMBERS

Bansi lived all of his ten years in the same little village in northern India. After his father died, his mother could barely earn enough for Bansi and his siblings to eat once a day. On some days, Bansi gave his portion of rice to his younger brother. In this grim existence, the only ray of hope for Bansi was the hope of meeting the region's ruler, the Rajah. This Rajah was extraordinarily wealthy and a heroic figure. All of the boys fantasized about being like the Rajah and dreamed of meeting him.

One day, the Rajah came to Bansi's village. The young boy ran up to the Rajah, who was seated on a huge elephant that knelt at the Rajah's command. Bansi said to the royal visitor, "Rajah, Rajah, I have waited so long to meet you! You are my hero! How can I serve you? What can I do for you?" The Rajah quietly looked Bansi over and finally said, "Give me your bag of rice." He was referring to the little pouch Bansi had tied around his waist. Bansi looked at the Rajah in anguished disbelief. How could the Rajah ask him for all he had in the world?

Bansi slowly handed his little bag of rice over to the Rajah, who took it and began to examine it carefully. Finally, when the tension was more than he could take, Bansi grabbed his pouch from the Rajah and ran back to his hut. He threw his bag against the wall of the hut and began to sob. Through his tears, he noticed that interspersed with his rice were small, shiny nuggets; the Rajah had been replacing the rice grain by grain with gold.

Gathering up the rice and the gold, Bansi ran back to the Rajah and said, "Rajah, Rajah, if I had only known what you were going to do with my rice, I would have given it all to you."

We have a Rajah, a King, who asks for all that we have and all that we are so that he can replace the common grains of rice that comprise our life now with the gold of lasting treasure. Jesus comes to us just as Gandalf came to Bilbo Baggins in *The Fellowship of the Ring* — not to rob him, but to help him by convincing him to give up his most cherished and most dangerous possession, the ring. Gandalf, the Rajah, and our Lord Jesus all unquestionably act out of love and goodness, but their desire to help must overcome our hearts of fear, possessiveness, greed, and pride.

Has the desire to "have it all" or the desire to protect the little we do have depleted our ability to pursue any single desire with deep passion? Does our striving for a "balanced life" actually prevent our achievement of it? Do the myriad calls to serve God prevent our hearing the clarion call to know God? Could it even be that our dedication to fulfill the Great Task[1] has left little energy to obey the Great Love[2]? Have our disappointments, failures, and losses clouded our vision of the One who alone brings hope, joy, and comfort? This book is an offer to focus and integrate scattered and fragmented lives. It is an invitation to simplicity in this age of complexity; a *compass* for the whole-life direction of those who realize that formulas for blessedness, recipes for success, and paths to holiness in five easy steps are at best deceptive and at worst fraudulent.

This book is for those who pursue the ascent when the trail steepens and the air thins, as well as for those hardy souls who have long hungered for the high mountain while yet wandering in the "misty lowlands."[3] It is for the busy who sense a deep yearning for the "one thing necessary," even as they are, like Martha, "worried and bothered about so many things" (Luke 10:41).

Even in the current Western culture of muchness and manyness, there are multitudes who struggle not with over-full lives but with empty ones. They have long since given up hope for ultimacy and intimacy, for meaning and relationship. For them it is unthinkable that there could be "one true thing" to fulfill all their dreams. But what if there is? This book is for them as well.

The One and the Many

The philosophical quest to find the one thing that lies behind all things in the universe is called the problem of "the one and the many." Basically stated, the problem of the one and the many begins from the assumption that, though it contains millions of components, ultimately the universe is one thing — a whole. Because it is itself a whole (one thing), there must be one unifying aspect behind the many things that exist or occur within it.

For most of us, the quest to find a unifying fabric for our lives is practical rather than philosophical. We are overwhelmed by the many and can't see the one forest for the many trees. We doubt whether the "one" even exists, and we consider suspect anyone who claims to have found an integrating point for all of life. People who give themselves to one thing are often viewed as obsessive, narrow-minded, or, worse yet, as fanatics. This view is accurate when it involves mindless dedication to a job, to a possession, to a cause, or even to a person. None of these are worthy of the human heart. They cannot bear the weight of such devotion.

But there is an insatiable and often unconscious hunger for "one thing" to make life work for me: something that will heal past wounds and failures; something to give relief to my pain; something to assuage my loneliness; something to bring joy, peace, and meaning. So as half-starved refugees, we attach our hope to and place our faith in whatever addresses the hungriest part of our souls. And that "whatever" is our god at that moment. To paraphrase John Calvin — a hungry and empty human heart is an idol-making factory.[4]

Becoming masters that enslave, these false hopes indeed emerge as "idols." So, to protect us from destructive idolatries, God gives priority of place to the commandment, "You shall have no other gods before Me" (Exodus 20:3). The first commandment pronounces there is only one true thing—the Living God, whom we know fully as revealed in Jesus Christ. To worship anything else is idolatry and foolishness. Not only is it sin, it is stupid. Did I say that strongly enough?

There can be any number of false "one things," but there is only one *true* thing that can deliver on the promise of unifying, integrating, and simplifying our lives.

A. W. Tozer powerfully describes the beauty and sanity of a life given to the one true thing:

> We need not fear that in seeking God only we may narrow our lives or restrict the motions of our expanding hearts.

The opposite is true. We can well afford to make God our All, to concentrate, to sacrifice the many for the One. . . . The man who has God for His treasure has all things in One. Many ordinary treasures may be denied him, or if he is allowed to have them, the enjoyment of them will be so tempered that they will never be necessary to his happiness. Or if he must see them go, one after one, he will scarcely feel a sense of loss, for having the Source of all things he has in One all satisfaction, all pleasure, all delight. Whatever he may lose he has actually lost nothing, for he now has it all in One, and he has it purely, legitimately and forever.[5]

Four centuries earlier, Francis de Sales anticipated Tozer as he encouraged the common folk of Geneva to believe that "the devotion which is true hinders nothing, but on the contrary it perfects everything."[6]

Tozer and de Sales are representative of the Christian spiritual ideology that encompasses all the traditions. It is one great river of devotion into which the Orthodox, Quaker, Wesleyan, Roman Catholic, Lutheran, Baptist, and Reformed tributaries flow. But in the last hundred years, the great rushing river has been dammed to a trickling stream — from wild to mild.

Someone pulled a fast one on us! We have been taken! Scammed! Deceived! We are not meant to be passive *consumers* of religious goods and services, but to be active participants in the pursuit of the one true thing.

The entire revelation of the Bible supports Tozer and de Sales, but nowhere more clearly than in the words of Jesus, "Seek first His kingdom and His righteousness, and all these things will be added to you" (Matthew 6:33). Seek the one, and the many will be taken care of.

But how many of us who name the name of Christ actually

believe that passionate devotion to God alone is the best life possible? How many of us even consider it a realistic possibility? We know we *should* believe it, so we profess it without believing it. We say, "Jesus is Lord," while we manage our lives apart from Him. We profess to be disciples of Jesus, but eagerly learn from almost anyone but Him when it comes to everyday living.

Let me tell you what I am up to. I want to change what you believe about God and about life. Why? Because you will always live out what you believe. Even the demons do as much, according to James 2:19. They believe and "shudder." If a person's only theology book was your life, what kind of god would they "read" about? Your life is the accurate statement of what you actually believe and, as they say, may be the only Bible some people ever read.

Feel guilty yet? Don't. I simply want you to begin thinking honestly about your beliefs. This is just the introduction. As Douglas Steere wrote in his introduction to *Purity of Heart Is to Will One Thing*, by Søren Kierkegaard (whom we'll get to know later), "In [Kierkegaard's] *Journals*, he makes a comment on the function of an introduction to a book. It should serve to unclothe the spectators from their diverse preoccupations and get them ready for the real bath."[7] So I hope you are beginning to feel a draft!

Where Are We Headed?

The following somewhat random yet connected statements will give you an idea of where we are going. It is only fair that you know our direction. And as the flight attendant says: If this isn't your destination, now would be an excellent time to get off the plane.

How do these thoughts strike you?

- The writer of Hebrews simply says, "All things are open and laid bare to the eyes of *Him with whom we have to do*"

(Hebrews 4:13, emphasis added).

- According to Oswald Chambers, "Jesus taught that a disciple has to make his relationship to God the dominating concentration of his life, and to be carefully careless about everything else in comparison to that."[8] We are liberated to be carefree in the care of God.
- The wellspring of life for the disciple is Jesus — all else is decoration or distraction.
- Jesus told the rich young ruler, "*One thing* you lack" (Mark 10:21, emphasis added). He was young. He was rich. He was in charge. He was religious. What could he possibly be lacking? Didn't he have everything? He had everything but the one true thing. How many times do we have to hear those who appear to have it all say, "There's got to be more to life than this," before we believe what our Bibles clearly teach?[9]
- In *My Utmost for His Highest*, Oswald Chambers states, "God nowhere tells us to give up things for the sake of giving them up. He tells us to give them up for the sake of the only thing worth having — viz., life with Himself."[10]
- Once a friend of mine asked what I think is the best question ever: Is Jesus enough? Right where I am, with what I have and who I am — is Jesus enough? If we ask this question when things are going well, we will be able to ask it when life is hard. And we will find, possibly to our surprise, that He is enough.
- Paul's fear for the Corinthians is my fear for myself and for those I love: "But I am afraid that, as the serpent deceived Eve by his craftiness, your minds will be led astray from the simplicity and purity of devotion to Christ" (2 Corinthians 11:3).
- C. S. Lewis, in his unparalleled description of the Christian faith, *Mere Christianity*, speaks of Jesus: "You can shut Him up as a fool, you can spit at Him and kill Him as a demon;

or you can fall at His feet and call Him Lord and God. But let us not come with any patronizing nonsense about His being a great human teacher. He has not left that open to us. He did not intend to."[11]

And that is the destination: at the feet of Jesus calling Him *my* Lord, *my* God, *my* one true thing.

How Are We Getting There?

We will be guided by a tenth-century-BC king, a fourteenth-century mystic, a first-century peasant woman, a nineteenth-century Danish philosopher, a converted Pharisee, and a sixteenth-century soldier turned contemplative missionary. What could that diverse group possibly have in common?

They found the life that is truly life (see 1 Timothy 6:19).

And that life is Jesus. Not Jesus and _____. Just the Jesus who said, "I am the way, and the truth, and the life" (John 14:6).

In case you haven't guessed, relationship/discipleship/apprenticeship to Jesus is the one true thing.

As you continue, you will discover three parts to this book. Within each part, the first chapter focuses on a biblical text, the second on a spiritual master from the past, and the third on Jesus' invitation to us.

Since most activities in life begin with desire, part 1 is about desiring and seeking the one thing. Desire leads to decision, so part 2 discusses choosing the one thing. When we choose in the same direction repeatedly, those choices become our character, our values. Part 3 describes what it means to value the one thing.

Well, I hope you haven't jumped off the plane and that you are ready to settle in for a leisurely yet adventurous journey toward the one true thing.

seeking

the

one

thing

A Pure and Holy Passion

One thing I have asked from the LORD, that I shall seek.

—PSALM 27:4

You can grow in knowledge if you take pains to set your heart
most upon one thing. That thing is nothing other than a
spiritual desire toward God—to please him, love him,
know him, here by grace in a little feeling, and in
the glory of heaven with a full being.

—WALTER HILTON

CHAPTER 1

Psalm 27

Seeking the One Thing over the Many

Whom have I in heaven but You?
And besides You, I desire nothing on earth.
— PSALM 73:25

There is only one desire and only one aspiration which fills the
poet's heart and in which all his other wishes converge and find their
fulfillment — that he may live in perpetual communion with God.
If he can have that, then he has everything.
— ARTUR WEISER

I have asked the Lord for many things.
How about you?

- I asked that the pretty little blonde in my kindergarten class
  would like me. (Didn't happen.)
- I asked to make the peewee football team. (Happened.)
- I asked to be the star of that team. (Didn't happen.)
- I asked that my dad would survive mouth and jaw cancer.
  (Happened.)
- I asked God to get me out of countless dilemmas in exchange
  for my empty promises of never sinning in that way again.
  (What do you think?)
- I asked to do well on exams for which I had not studied.
  (Didn't happen.)

- With two outs and the game tied in the bottom of the ninth inning in the state high school championship game, I asked to get on base. (Happened.)
- I asked for just the right woman to become my wife and be the love of my life. (Happened!)
- I asked for perfect kids with straight teeth who never got into trouble. (Didn't happen.)

When I have asked — when you have asked — for many things, the common context is need. Sometimes the need is as trivial as success in a ball game. At other times, it is life and death. But, regardless of the context, those of us who profess to know God ask.

This is a good thing. God is the giver of every good gift (see James 1:17). Jesus tells us to ask and to seek, because the generosity of our heavenly Father far outstrips that of any earthly father (see Matthew 7:7-11). After all, the Father gave us His Son. We can be sure that He will not withhold from us any good thing.

So as we dive into Psalm 27 to look at asking for the one thing, there is no reason to stop asking our gracious heavenly Father for whatever it is that we need. God delights for us to come to Him as dependent children. However, we will learn from this psalm that it is possible to subjugate our many requests to the one great request.

Then we will find along with A. W. Tozer that "for all God's good will toward us He is unable to grant us our heart's desires till all our desires have been reduced to one."[1]

Absolute Prayer from Absolute Poverty

Context is everything. If I say "I do" in reply to the harmless question, "Do you want mustard on that burger?" I am a little happier about my lunch. But if I say "I do" in a church in front of a minister, and I am standing next to a woman dressed in white, it will have lifelong impact. Context matters.

In this amazing psalm, David said, "One thing I have asked from the LORD, that I shall seek" (Psalm 27:4). What was the context for his bold statement? Was it a moment of reflection as he rested comfortably in his palace surrounded by his servants, subjects, and soldiers? Possibly it was a moment of triumph after winning another huge battle as Yahweh's anointed king. It even could have been an ecstatic moment after he had retreated to a secret hideaway to play his harp, pray, and write a few psalms.

But it is none of these. The words of Psalm 27 accurately give the context: evildoers, devour, adversaries, enemies, war, trouble, forsaken, foes, false witnesses, violence. David is not speaking from the safety of the palace or from the sanctity of the temple or from the seat of power. As you read John Calvin's description of the context, imagine the thoughts and feelings you would have if you were in David's situation:

> Although David was banished from his country, despoiled of his wife, bereft of his kinsfolk; and, finally, dispossessed of his substance, yet he was not so desirous for the recovery of these, as he was grieved and afflicted for his banishment from God's sanctuary, and the loss of his sacred privileges. Under the word *one*, there is an implied antithesis, in which David, disregarding all other interests, displays his intense affection for the service of God; so that it was bitterer for him to be an exile from the sanctuary, than to be denied access to his own house.[2]

In summary, David has lost everything. Calvin places this psalm's setting in the midst of Absalom's rebellion — the son usurping the father's throne. David has nothing left except one thing: a desperate desire for God. *This* is what it means to be a person after God's own heart.

Having lost everything, David doesn't curse God. Instead, he *wants* God.

Having been betrayed by family and friends, he doesn't blame God. Rather, he *seeks* God.

Having been confronted by merciless human ugliness, he doesn't forsake God. He *longs* for the beauty of God.

We must pause for a moment here and accept the fact that David was a real human person — more like us than not. In the psalm, David wrote about his mother and father forsaking him. Who among us has not experienced family pain and conflict? For some, the betrayal is as subtle as love and approval withheld. For others, it is tragic neglect or abuse. Many of us have experienced the deep wound of not being loved well by those whose primary responsibility it was to do just that. Such is the wound of betrayal David experienced.

My best guess of when this happened in David's life is when he was a young shepherd boy and the prophet Samuel paid his father Jesse a visit. Samuel was looking to anoint one of Jesse's sons as king, so Jesse lined them all up in front of Samuel — except David. David was out in the fields tending the sheep, and his father did not send for him. What must that have felt like for David? When he found out, he must have been angry and hurt — the kind of hurt that stings for a lifetime and screams for revenge. But David didn't wallow in his pain, nor did he strike back in bitterness. He simply turned to the God he knew *could not* betray him.

What sort of a person had he become that he could seek God alone, "disregarding all other interests"? How did he manage in the midst of absolute poverty to pray the absolute prayer? We must also pause for each of us to ask the question, "Is this the kind of person I would like to be?"

As you reflect on those questions, consider this aspect of David's character: the undivided heart. In Psalm 86 David asks God, "Unite my heart to fear Your name" (verse 11). And just before his death he challenges his son Solomon to "wholehearted devotion" to God (1 Chronicles 28:9, NIV). David, like us, made inexcusable mistakes. David, like us, hurt and was hurt by those he loved. David, like us, knew the heights of joy and the depths of despair.

But, unlike most of us, through it all, with an undivided heart, he wanted God more than anything.

Another Context

As we ask ourselves the question, "How did David come to the place of desiring the one thing?" it will help to notice an additional context of Psalm 27. Not only were sin and evil present in full force, but so was God. And this was the context that defined reality for David.

Psalm 27 begins with the acknowledgment that the Lord is our light and our salvation. It is not so startling for David, or for us, to see God as our only hope of deliverance from trouble. He is our hope here and in the hereafter; that is, for our salvation. But in what sense is the Lord to be our "light"?

Think about what light does. It allows us to see everything else. In a dark room, not only can I not see light, I cannot see anything. While visiting the incredible hewn-rock churches in Lalibela, Ethiopia, we were guided into a stone tunnel that connected two of the churches. For centuries, this tunnel has been called the "seventh degree of hell" because of its pitch darkness. I put my hand an inch from my eye and still could not see it. That is life without God.

Goodness, truth, and beauty can be right in front of us, but without God as light, we don't even notice. Only because of God can I "see" others, myself, and reality. With a "God is my light" context, everything else comes into focus. Because this was the lens through which David looked at all of life, he saw clearly the necessity, rightness, and wisdom of asking for "one thing" and only one thing.

One Thing, Three Verbs

Happily, we are not left to imagine what asking for the one thing looks like. The psalm gives us three lively verbs in verse 4 that flesh out the skeletal idea of seeking the one thing.

That I May Dwell in the House of the LORD All the Days of My Life

This request is not for a perpetual church service. David's one yearning is for the Presence of Yahweh, experienced acutely in the temple (the house of the Lord) but not limited to it. David expresses here his faith that the Presence of God provides everything he needs. It makes all other concerns, dangers, troubles, losses, and pains of this life seem secondary. As long as God was with him, he knew he could endure whatever might come his way — "whom shall I fear?" (verse 1). Such is the strength and courage of those friends of God who have long since settled the question of God's faithful presence with them.

The elusive "with-God life" that David longed for, asked for, and sought is now freely given and guaranteed to all who put their confidence in Jesus, who is Immanuel, God with us. But do I really want this "with-God life"?[3]

One does not have to read far into any of the Gospels to notice that the presence of Jesus not only brought comfort to the troubled but also troubled the comfortable. Living life in the presence of

God is entering into a dimension where Jesus is Lord and I am not. It is a place where what God wants done gets done — whether that is in my heart, in my relationships, in my activities, in my possessions, or in my body.

But mainly what God wants done is freedom for the captives, healing for the brokenhearted, sight for the blind, and good news proclaimed to those who are "down and out." In other words, His kingdom come, His will be done on earth as it is done in heaven (see Matthew 6:10).

To Behold the Beauty of the LORD

David had a sense of the majestic beauty of the God who is the source of all beauty, creativity, and enjoyment. It is beauty that arouses desire and sustains devotion. When David caught a glimpse of the ark of the covenant being brought into Jerusalem, he expressed his overflowing desire and devotion by dancing. Awareness of beauty does that — even to a warrior king.

Anyone who has lost his desire for God has first lost the vision of God's magnificence, brilliance, and radiant glory. If you find your desire for God waning, look at Jesus. Fix your eyes on Him.

Join Mary of Bethany in sitting at His feet, listening to His voice, and looking full into His wonderful face.

Join the crowds who beheld the beauty of His grace as He forgave the terrified woman who had been caught in adultery. Look on in awe with those who beheld the beauty of His power as He fed the five thousand and the beauty of His compassion as He touched lepers, gave sight to the blind, and blessed those who were thought to be "unblessable."

Join Nicodemus, the woman at the well, and the disciples in beholding the beauty of the life of Jesus. They experienced what

C. S. Lewis described as the deep desire of the human heart: "We do not want merely to *see* beauty. We want something else which can hardly be put into words — to be united with the beauty we see, to pass into it, to receive it into ourselves, to bathe in it, to become part of it."[4]

We can look at Jesus only for so long without His beauty stirring our desire to know Him. As we "grow in the grace and knowledge of our Lord and Savior Jesus Christ" (2 Peter 3:18), we inevitably step closer to an undistracted devotion to Him.[5] And this is where we become part of the beauty of who He is — Christ formed in us.[6]

To Meditate in His Temple

Here David's desire is to meditate upon the beauty he has seen in the presence of the Lord. The Hebrew word for meditate, *hagah*, means "chew" or "gnaw" — as a lion over its prey. Just as what the lion "meditates" on becomes part of him, so when we meditate, chew on, the beauty of the Lord, it passes into us and becomes part of us.

The location of choice for David is the physical temple that he has been exiled from. But in the Psalms, the temple of the Lord extends far beyond a building to include all of creation.[7] Therefore, David's meditation is not limited by location, but can take place anywhere.

The lesson for us is obvious. We don't need a quiet place, a sanctuary, or a retreat center in which to meditate. All we need to do is slow down right where we are and reflect on the meaning of what we are experiencing as we stand in the presence of the Lord and behold His beauty.

It is meditation that allows us to notice and respond to the fire of God's presence, voice, and action in the midst of the ordinariness of our lives. The acts of abiding, beholding, and meditating are the responses of those who have asked for the one thing. One scholar, commenting on Psalm 27, speaks of David's kind of total devotion this way:

> Only he can speak thus who has given up all dependence on his fellow men and above all on himself in exchange for an exclusive dependence on God which is unconditional and accepted without any reservation whatsoever. That inward independence of anything which is human makes a man truly free from any kind of fear, but is only granted to him to whom God means everything and for whom God is the ultimate goal in the actual practical circumstances of his life.[8]

Sometimes we must come to the place, as David did, where God is all we have, in order to recognize that God is all we need.

On one of the great battlefields of the Civil War, the body of a young, unidentified soldier was found. The search through his pockets yielded a scribbling that has been handed down as "The Prayer of the Unknown Confederate Soldier." It captures the essence and beauty of asking for the one thing:

> *I asked God for strength, that I might achieve;*
> *I was made weak, that I might learn humbly to obey.*
> *I asked for health, that I might do greater things;*
> *I was given infirmity that I might do better things.*
> *I asked for riches, that I might be happy;*
> *I was given poverty, that I might be wise.*
> *I asked for power, that I might have the praise of men;*
> *I was given weakness, that I might feel the need of God.*
> *I asked for all things, that I might enjoy life;*

I was given life, that I might enjoy all things.
I got nothing that I asked for — but everything I had
hoped for.
Almost despite myself, my unspoken prayers were answered.
I among all men, am most richly blessed.[9]

CHAPTER 2

Julian of Norwich

The Life of Seeking the One Thing

> God, of your goodness give me yourself, for you are enough for me,
> and I can ask for nothing which is less which can pay you full worship.
> And if I ask anything which is less, always I am in want;
> but only in you do I have everything.
> — JULIAN OF NORWICH

We need heroes to inspire us toward the Life, and we need willing models to show us the Way. We need those living the Truth who will say to us, as the apostle Paul said to his friends, "Follow me as I follow Christ" (1 Corinthians 11:1, PAR). Occasionally God provides one person in whom all three needs are met.

The fourteenth-century anchoress[1] Julian of Norwich is one of those rare saints. Her radical life and her sacrificial love for Jesus clearly qualify her for heroine status. But can this humble mystic from six hundred years ago possibly be a model for twenty-first-century Christians? I am convinced that she *must* be. As you read on, I think you will agree.

James Snyder reports that A. W. Tozer, the God-pursuing evangelical pastor of the early twentieth century, affectionately referred to Julian as his "girlfriend."[2] Today, he probably would have called her his "soul mate." He recognized in her a kindred spirit who shared his passionate thirst for God.

In the description below, Kelby Cotton describes Julian, though he could as easily have been describing Julian's admirer Tozer:

> How rare it is to find a person that combines the qualities of deep theological insight and a profound poetic sensibility. How unusual to find one who considers seriously her mystical experiences and yet never leaves behind an earthy common sense. How delightful to discover one who takes God so seriously that all else is taken lightly and with uncommon grace and gratitude. Just such a woman is Julian of Norwich.[3]

Tozer and Julian on the surface would seem to be a mismatched couple, but lines of denomination and dogma become blurred in the presence of those who take Jesus with ultimate seriousness and all other things with appropriate lightness and grace. There is infinite common ground for those who desire Jesus above all.

Who Was Julian of Norwich?

Few historical facts are available concerning this amazing woman. We do not even know her name. St. Julian's in Norwich, England, was the church to which she "anchored" herself and from which her name is derived. She lived from 1342 until roughly 1413 and spent most of that time in her cell attached to the church. Typically, an anchoress's cell would have a window into the church, through which she could participate in worship, and a window to the world, through which she would offer spiritual direction to those who came to her.

Anne Savage and Nicholas Watson tell us that anchorites and anchoresses

- lived their lives "permanently enclosed in cells which were attached to churches and . . . , as a result, usually lived in the middle of villages or towns";[4]

- viewed their vocation as a "living death" — an idea that plays a central role in the enclosure ceremony, in which the priest administers the last rites and "recites prayers for the dying as she or he enters the anchorhouse — never, in theory, to leave it alive";[5]
- lived through "much of the year on one meal a day, strictly observing all the church's fasts" and spent most of each day in silence;[6]
- took care to treat those on the outside with courtesy, for they were "dependent on the charity of others for food";[7]
- sacrificed their own comfort, and often their own health, to embrace "a way of life of the most extreme heroism and holiness";[8]
- sought to share "in Christ's physical and moral sufferings, by enduring poverty, pain, and humiliation, and by battling with the spiritual sins." It was their fundamental "hope to become like him in this life, and also to share more fully in his joy in the next";[9]
- turned their backs on "the world, physical comfort and the pleasure of sexual intimacy," embracing instead "a heroic and anxious struggle against their own sinful nature and the promptings of the devil, . . . not only for the hope of a high heavenly reward — although that is a strong motive — but for a union with Christ . . . which begins here, in this life.[10]

Such a life was God-intoxicated, Spirit-filled, and Jesus-centered discipleship in full flower. It is what Paul referred to when he wrote, "You have died and your life is hidden with Christ in God" (Colossians 3:3) and "I have been crucified with Christ; and it is no longer I who live, but Christ lives in me" (Galatians 2:20). One of the most important things to be said about the anchoritic life is that it was meant to embody these spiritual transformations in a highly physical and public way.

It is only fitting that Julian of Norwich's work survived, making her the first woman writer recorded in English-language history. Even more appropriate is that she wrote about her desire for Jesus and how that desire was fulfilled.

The *Showings*

In her mid-thirties, Julian became so ill that last rites were administered to her. One night, as she lay on the brink of death, she was given sixteen visions or "showings" that imparted to her an experience of union with Christ that few have ever known. By the morning, she was completely healed and would spend the rest of her life meditating, praying, and writing about her visions of Jesus.

There are two versions of *Showings*. The first is the short text, written soon after her near-death experience, that briefly reports what she saw. Twenty years later, after much prayer and reflection, she wrote the long text.

Even in that detail she modeled something important for us. Do we simply move from experience to experience, relationship to relationship, task to task, and insight to insight without ever pausing to explore their meanings? Is that how it is possible to have such full lives and such empty souls at the same time?

For years Julian asked many times what the Lord meant for her to learn from what she had experienced. It is refreshing that, though her life was very different from ours, she asked similar questions. The answer she received was, "What, do you wish to know your Lord's meaning in this thing? Know it well, love was his meaning. Who reveals it to you? Love. What did he reveal to you? Love. Why does he reveal it to you? For love. Remain in this, and you will know more of the same. But you will never know different, without end."[11] In the love of God alone, we find the meaning of life, of our lives, and of all existence.

For Julian and her fellow seekers, this one thing provides the sieve through which to filter all of life and even impending death. It provides a unifying, integrating, and simplifying point of meaning, a universal for the mass of particulars that make up our lives.

Julian's relentless desire for union and communion with Jesus was expressed by the unusual word *one-ing*. It brings together the active and passive components of union with Christ. It is what Julian called "longing with my will for God."[12] It is passive in that it reflects the soul's desire and longing. It is active in that the intensity of the desire engages the will in seeking. Others have referred to it as "holy intention." In Julian's words,

> God judges us in our natural substance, which is always kept one in him, whole and safe, without end; and this judgment is out of his justice. And man judges us in our changeable sensuality, which now seems one thing and now another, as it derives from parts and presents an external appearance. . . . The first judgment, which is from God's justice, is from his own great endless love, and that is that fair, sweet judgment which was shown in all the fair revelation in which I saw him assign to us no kind of blame.[13]

Julian was recklessly abandoned to God's "great endless love" because she had seen it graphically in her visions of Jesus. Love like that could "assign to us no kind of blame."

That is the good news. God is not judging us based on the outward appearance of changeable performance or halting faithfulness, but rather on the inward character of a heart united to Him through Jesus. Indeed, it is "man [who] looks at the outward appearance, but the LORD looks at the heart" (1 Samuel 16:7).

This freedom from fear of judgment released her, as a medieval woman in a male-dominated society, to risk writing what the Lord had shown her. She could not keep this love that she had experienced to herself. Reception and experience of the perfect love of God extinguishes our fear of human judgment and reprisal.

Even as I write this, I wrestle with fears of what you, my unknown reader, may think of me. Resting in God's love, I am free to write my heart. But trapped in fear, I try to use words to impress and to win approval. Live in love or live in fear. Those are my options. Julian shows me the "more excellent way" (1 Corinthians 12:31) of love.

Julian, as an anchoress, lived in her anchorhold — the symbol of her devotion to one-ing. Our desire, our holy intention, not our performance, is our "anchorhold." The anchorhold is a place of desire and love. With performance as my anchorhold, I may enjoy the thrill of "measuring up" for a while. However, it won't be long before the thrill turns to fear and I completely lose sight of the one thing.

How then does Julian's one-ing help us desire and seek the one thing? Her desire for union with Christ was expressed in her prayer for three wounds: "the wound of true contrition, the wound of loving compassion, and the wound of longing with my will for God."[14] These were the means through which she could be crucified with Christ and participate in His risen life. They were means of dying to self and living to God. Her "wounds" can be our healing if we have the courage to ask as Julian did.

One-ing Through True Contrition

In the words she wrote, Julian demonstrated the true contrition she prayed for:

- I counsel you for your own profit, that you disregard the

wretch to whom [the revelation] was shown, and that mightily, wisely, and meekly you contemplate on God, who out of his courteous love and his endless goodness was willing to show it generally, to the comfort of us all.

- I am not good because of the revelations, but only if I love God better;
- For I am sure that there are many who never had revelations or visions, but only the common teaching of the church, who love God better than I.[15]

True contrition is a sane estimate of my inner person before God. Julian doesn't deny through a false modesty that she has been blessed with an incredible gift in the revelations that she received. Rather, in the way of all true mystics, she directs the attention to the Giver's love and goodness.

True contrition not only openly acknowledges present sin, it also anticipates future progress in holiness. It inflames my desire to love God "better" than I do now.

True contrition prevents comparison to others by keeping me deeply connected both to my own sinful inadequacy and to God's more-than-adequate grace. Aware of my own weaknesses, I dare not compare. Receptive to God's unconditional love, I don't need to compare.

True contrition is a synonym for our contemporary word *brokenness*. Loving produces brokenness. Out of love Jesus emptied Himself, became one of us, and was broken for us. Any time I truly love as Jesus did, the odds are good that I will be broken as Jesus was by rejection, by misunderstanding, by neglect, by cruel circumstances. Even as I love God, I am broken on the rock of His holiness, His mystery, His utter freedom, and finally on the enormous rock of His love — love that I can never fully requite.

In all of these, one-ing occurs as my desire for God increases.

I see Him as the Source of all goodness, healing, growth, love—everything I want and need.

True contrition is one-ing inward toward the God who is love.

One-ing Through Loving Compassion

Julian's fourteenth-century world was torn by the Black Plague, assassinations, incredible violence, war, and social unrest. Understandably, there was a climate of fear and a questioning of God's love and mercy.

In that dismal culture, Julian boldly stood against the brooding pessimism with a buoyant yet well-grounded optimism. She corrected misperceptions about her "courteous Lord" with statements such as, "He did not say: You will not be troubled, you will not be belaboured, you will not be disquieted; but he said: You will not be overcome."[16] And again, "for it is his will that we know that all the power of the enemy is shut in the hand of our Friend."[17]

She was no flighty "Pollyanna" pretending that pain and evil weren't a threat. But her experience with Jesus gave her a settled faith that resurrection is the backdrop for crucifixion, that suffering is the prelude to glory, and that pain is an opportunity for redemption.

In her words, "And at the end of woe, suddenly our eyes will be opened, and in the clearness of our sight our light will be full, which light is God, our Creator, Father, and the Holy Spirit, in Christ Jesus our Savior. So I saw and understood that our faith is our light in our night, which light is God, our endless day."[18]

Her compassion in dealing with the sin of others flows directly from the three wounds that she asked God for: "We cannot see the beauty of God, unless we contemplate [a person's sins] with contrition with him, with compassion on him, and with holy desires to God for him."[19] Even as she ministered to others with compassion, she stepped back into her own one-ing toward God.

The pain and suffering that she saw around her was an occasion to realize that there was nothing outside the reaches of God's love. She heard her "courteous Lord" say, "I may make all things well, and I can make all things well, and I shall make all things well; and you will see yourself that every kind of thing will be made well."[20]

Loving compassion is one-ing outward to find Jesus in those He loves, especially in the least, the last, and the lost.

One-ing Through Willful Longing for God

This third desire Julian asked for unconditionally, urgently, and continually. By her own admission, the desire to long for God with her will was her primary means of one-ing.

Here she found deep consolation and painful desolation:

- Ah, Lord Jesus, king of bliss, how shall I be comforted, who will tell me and teach me what I need to know, if I cannot at this time see it in you?[21]
- Always, the more clearly that the soul sees the blessed face by the grace of loving, the more it longs to see it in fullness, that is to say in God's own likeness . . . for in that precious sight no woe can remain, no well-being can be lacking.[22]
- Still we should never cease to mourn and to weep in the spirit, because, that is, of our painful longing, until we might see our Creator's fair blessed face.[23]

In this longing, Julian counsels us toward seeking and waiting. These are the two sides of the coin of surrender. We surrender our wills by intentional, grace-assisted, yet diligent application of our wills to seek God above all else. This is done through the intelligent and well-directed application of spiritual disciplines.[24]

We also surrender by harnessing our wills into waiting and contemplating. For many, this passivity is more challenging than the activity. Here we are called to surrender control, timing, direction, and ultimately our own ego's needs and desires. We empty ourselves and wait to be filled by our gracious Lord. As difficult as this can be, true longing for God cannot happen without it.

But it is more than worth the surrendering, seeking, and waiting, as Julian boldly proclaims:

> And also God in his special grace visits whom he will with such great contrition, and also with compassion and true longing for him, that they are suddenly delivered from sin and from pain, and take up into bliss and made equal with the saints. By contrition we are made clean, by compassion we are made ready, and by true longing for God we are made worthy. These are three means, as I understand, through which all souls come to heaven, those, that is to say, who have been sinners on earth and will be saved.[25]

True longing for God is one-ing upward to discover the face of Jesus in our deep desire. The prayer of the sixth-century Celtic ascetic Columbanus shows us how to ask for the one thing: "Loving Saviour, be pleased to show yourself to us who knock, so that in knowing you we may love only you, love you alone, desire you alone, contemplate only you day and night, and always think of you."[26]

CHAPTER 3

Jesus' Invitation to Seek the One Thing

"What do you want?"
— JOHN 1:38 (NIV)

My Lord God, my all in all, life of my life, and spirit of my spirit,
look in mercy upon me and so fill me with thy Holy Spirit that my
heart shall have no room for love of aught but thee. I seek from
thee no other gift but thyself, who are the Giver of life and all its
blessings. From thee I ask not for the world or its treasures, nor yet
for heaven even make request, but thee alone do I desire
and long for; and where thou art, there is heaven.
— SADHU SUNDAR SINGH

There is only one being who can satisfy the last aching abyss of
the human heart, and that is the Lord Jesus Christ.
— OSWALD CHAMBERS

What is it that *you* want?

Jesus — Master of Life, brilliant teacher, amazing psychologist — asks the ultimate question then and now: "What are you seeking?" (John 1:38, ESV). Why this question? Because what I seek determines what I choose, and what I choose forms my values, which equal who I am. Jesus moves directly to the hidden bedrock of our lives with this question. While we dabble on the surfaces of outward appearance, God in the flesh drills deeply to look upon the heart.

To be human and alive is to be seeking, to have desires for our lives. Too often, religion has been concerned with "stamping out" desires rather than demonstrating how every human yearning at its core is a desire for God. As the truism states, "A man knocking on the door of a brothel is looking for God."[1] He is just looking in the wrong place.

This is what Jesus is doing with His question — helping us connect our desire, our seeking, with its only worthy object. Jesus understood that "the desire after God and holiness is back of all real spirituality, and when that desire becomes dominant in the life nothing can prevent us from having what we want."[2]

He invites our desire. . . .

Let Anyone Who Is Thirsty Come to Me

The Feast of Tabernacles was, in part, a reminder of Israel's forty years of living in tents in the wilderness, where God brought them manna from heaven and water from the rock. On the last day of the feast, which occurred at the end of the dry season, thousands of pilgrims would jam the temple courts and pray to God for life-giving rain. The chorus of cries would have been almost deafening as the people shouted to God, "Hosannah! Hosannah! Save us! Send us rain!"[3]

Throughout the weeklong ceremonies, "living water" was a central part of the ritual, as the priest would draw water with a golden pitcher from the Pool of Siloam, which was filled by the Spring of Gihon. The Israelites knew two kinds of water: stale and dirty cistern water that collected after a rain; and living water, which was fresh, naturally flowing spring water.

The prophet Jeremiah emphasized the symbolism of these two kinds of water:

For My people have committed two evils:
They have forsaken Me,
The fountain of living waters,

To hew for themselves cisterns,
Broken cisterns
That can hold no water. (Jeremiah 2:13)

But thirst can make us desperate for any kind of water. We start hewing for ourselves the cisterns of self-sufficiency, self-assertion, and self-help. The stagnant pools that collect there contain the stale water of religiosity, self-righteousness, pride, or idolatry.

In that context, on the last day of the feast and as if in response to their prayers, Jesus offered far more than simple H_2O: "If anyone is thirsty, let him come to Me and drink" (John 7:37). He goes on to make the almost unthinkable claim that out of their "innermost being will flow rivers of living water" (verse 38). This is the "once in a lifetime," "win the lottery" "offer you can't refuse" kind of invitation.

They were saying their routine prayers for rain, but instead their souls were flooded with the offer to drink and overflow with *living* water. The unique water of relationship with Jesus satisfies the deepest thirsts of our souls yet leaves us wanting more of Jesus. Thirteenth-century contemplative Gertrude the Great experienced this vividly: "Ah, Jesus, fountain of life, make me drink a cup of the living water from you so that, having tasted you, I will thirst eternally for nothing but you."[4]

When I am thirsty, it is not enough to see the water, or touch the water, or know about the water, or even give water to others. Unless I actually drink, I will remain thirsty. But when I do drink, I "taste and see that the LORD is good" (Psalm 34:8). It is the *experience* of having my thirsty desires satisfied by Jesus that changes my heart and helps me face the continual challenge of allowing the desire for God to dominate. As Lewis observed,

We are half-hearted creatures fooling about with drink and sex and ambition when infinite joy is offered us, like an ignorant child who wants to go on making mudpies in a slum because he cannot imagine what is meant by the offer of a holiday at sea. We are far too easily pleased.[5]

But one sip of the living water makes us see the mudpies for what they are — dirty little distractions.

Henri Nouwen, one of the most profound spiritual writers of the twentieth century, said it this way:

> What do we really desire? As I try to listen to my own deepest yearning as well as to the yearnings of others, the word that seems best to summarize the desire of the human heart is "communion." . . . God has given us a heart that will remain restless until it has found full communion. We look for it in sexual intimacy, in moments of ecstasy, in the recognition of our gifts. We look for it through success, admiration, and rewards. But wherever we look, it is communion we seek.[6]

And it is not simply communion with friends, spouses, family, or coworkers that we seek, but a oneness with ourselves and the Transcendent. We long for intimacy and ultimacy. Again, Nouwen puts it sharply, "Our desire for God is the desire that should guide all other desires."[7]

What Do I Really Want?

I sometimes wonder why God isn't giving me what I want. The old Scottish pastor and poet George MacDonald offers an explanation: "Man finds it hard to get what he wants, because he does not want the best; God finds it hard to give, because He would give the best, and man will not take it."[8]

And this is the great danger: not that we should fail or fall dramatically, but that we would succeed in misguided quests. While Jesus offers the refreshing water of Life in the Kingdom, we are tempted to settle for the stagnant pools of life in our own kingdoms — financial security, congenial friends, religious activities, and pleasurable diversions.

Evelyn Underhill points to our only hope of rescue: "From our distorted life 'unquieted with dreads, bound with cares, busied with vanities, vexed with temptations' the soul in its prayer reaches out to center its trust on the Eternal, the existent."[9]

According to Oswald Chambers, "There is nothing easier than getting into a right relationship with God except when it is not God Whom you want but only what He gives."[10] When Jesus said, "Seek first the kingdom of God" (Matthew 6:33, ESV), He must have known that adding "and all these things will be added to you" would cloud the issue for us. But He also knew that it would require us to clarify what it is that we are seeking. If I am truly seeking first the Kingdom, then I could not care less about whatever might be added beyond that. When I am convinced that "he who has God and everything has no more than he who has God alone,"[11] I am no longer driven by the desire to take care of myself. I am freed to trust God.

That is the force of Jesus' words in Matthew 16:25: "For those who want to save their life will lose it, and those who lose their life for my sake will find it" (NRSV). Jesus again speaks to the hidden wants and desires from which our choices emerge. Is the controlling energy within me that of self-protection and self-preservation? Do I want to save my own life? Or is there a deeper desire in me to give up the project of running my own life and recklessly abandon myself to Jesus?

God, who has put desires into our hearts, uses those desires as mile markers to direct us to the one true desire. God's desire is for us — God wants us more than we want God. God is the initiator and the pursuer. So Jesus invites us to come and drink, come and rest, come and follow. He is constantly knocking on the door of our heart (see Revelation 3:20), and often the knocks we hear first are our own desires for "more" — more love, more peace, more joy, more friends, more money, more meaning, more life.

And make no mistake, it is God who is at work stirring up our hopes, frustrating our selfish ambitions, and salting our thirst for the living water.

The saints of old knew that their own desires fell short of the great and perfect gifts God wanted to give, so they prayed,

> Teach me to seek you, and when I seek you show yourself to me, for I cannot seek you unless you teach me, nor can I find you unless you show yourself to me. Let me seek you in desiring you and desire you in seeking you, let me find you by loving you, and love you in finding you.[12]

God, in absolute humility, takes on the role of the lovesick pursuer seeking His beloved gently yet relentlessly, longing to be sought in return. A. W. Tozer, a passionate modern seeker, expresses the response our Lord looks for: "We pursue God because, and only because, He has first put an urge within us that spurs us to the pursuit. . . . the outworking of that impulse is our following hard after Him."[13]

Where Does Desire for God Come From?

Just as we love only because God first loved us, we desire God only because God has first desired us. The French spiritual master Jean-Pierre de Caussade wrote that God "wishes to be alone the food of our heart, the sole object of our desiring."[14]

The desire of the psalmist, too, is deep and passionate:

How lovely are Your dwelling places, O LORD of hosts!
My soul longed and even yearned for the courts of the
    LORD;
My heart and my flesh sing for joy to the living God.
    (Psalm 84:1-2)

There is yearning and longing here. From where does this rumbling desire arise? It erupts from the *vision* of the goodness and joy of life in the presence of the Lord. The royal court would have been the place of supreme beauty, art, and opulence, as well as power. It was the place to be. Now imagine the courts of the Lord. What soul wouldn't yearn to be in the place of infinite goodness, beauty, truth, and power? This is the throne room that followers of Jesus are invited to boldly enter. Can you see it? Before you will desire it, you have to see it.

- When I *see* that life with Jesus is the best life I can imagine, then I will long and yearn for that life.
- When I *see* Jesus as the brilliant Master of Life, then I will want to learn from Him.
- When I *see* God wildly in love with me, then I will want to love God.
- When I *see* that my heavenly Father cares for the birds of the air and the lilies of the field and considers me of greater worth than those, then I will want to surrender to the Father's care for me.
- When I *see* following Jesus as life's hidden treasure, then I will want to sacrifice anything and everything to get it.

Desire is the fruit of vision, and unfortunately the best among us now "see in a mirror dimly"; but there will come a time when we will see "face to face" (1 Corinthians 13:12). For now, the best way

I know to clean the mirrors of our vision is to focus on Jesus in the Gospels. Let the generous and varied pictures of Him in the gospel stories escort you into wide-eyed wonder. Before you know it, you will be consumed with desire for your gracious Lord.

The crucial, life-determining question then becomes not "*What* do you want?" but "*Who* do you want?" In fact, this is the question the risen Jesus asked Mary Magdalene: "Whom are you seeking?" (John 20:15). Mary's answer, which can be clearly deduced from her words and actions, was simply, "Jesus."

When this is our answer, we are immediately catapulted into the category of spiritual leader. For in a world where many who speak for God are like travel agents handing out glossy brochures to places they have never seen, those who seek the one thing are set apart by their humble authenticity. How big a deal is this? Read this historical observation and decide for yourself:

> In the early centuries of the Christian church, the primary focus of the education of the priest or pastor was on spiritual or character formation. . . . The early church fathers and mothers were concerned that persons not assume the clerical office if they lacked the necessary spiritual maturity, even though they may possess knowledge and skills. On balance the primary qualification for ordination in antiquity was to possess the *desire for God*.[15] (emphasis added)

The desire for God that sums up our asking, seeking, and yearning is expressed in this prayer of Anselm — theologian, doctor of the church, and man of prayer:

> *I love you, O my God; and I desire to love you more and more.*
> *Grant to me that I may love you as much as I desire, and as*
> *much as I ought. O dearest Friend, who has loved and saved*

*me, the thought of whom is so sweet and always growing
sweeter, watch over my lips, my steps, my deeds, and I shall
not need to be anxious either for my soul or my body. Give me
love, sweetest of all gifts, which knows no enemy. Give me in
my heart pure love, born of your love to me, that I may love
others as you love me. O most loving Father of Jesus Christ,
from whom flows all love, let my heart, frozen in sin, cold to
you and cold to others, be warmed by this divine fire. So help
and bless me in your Son. Amen.*[16]

choosing

the

one

thing

A Magnificent Obsession

"Only one thing is necessary, for Mary has chosen
the good part."

— LUKE 10:42

CHAPTER 4

Luke 10:38-42

Choosing the One Thing over the Many

Put first things first and we get second things thrown in: put second
things first and we lose both first things and second things.
— C. S. LEWIS

Julian of Norwich moved from desiring to deciding, from seeking
to choosing, from visions to disciplines. The ecstasy of desire led
her into the routine of daily choices. It matters little to what heights
desire may carry us if the depths of our real life remain unaffected.
It is true, I suppose, that the road to hell is paved with good inten-
tions . . . but so is the road to heaven. My daily decisions become the
mechanism of translating my holy intention into holy living.

Understanding this, William Law wrote, "If we are to be in
Christ new creatures, we must show that we are so, by having new
ways of living in the world. If we are to follow Christ it must be in
our common way of spending every day."[1] Our discipleship to Jesus
is for our whole life and for our real life. We live with and in Jesus.

The apostle Paul emphasized the importance of a daily walk
with Christ in his letter to the Colossians: "As therefore you received
Christ Jesus the Lord, so live in him" (Colossians 2:6, RSV). The
Greek word behind *live* has the basic meaning of "walk around." We
all once "walked around" in sin and idolatry (see Colossians 3:5-7),
but now, since we "received" Jesus, we "walk around" in Him. I like

the ordinariness of that word. In the contemporary vernacular, we might use the term *hang out*. Once I enter a relationship with Jesus, His desire is that I "hang out" with Him 24/7 for the rest of my life. And that is something I can learn to do, if I so choose.

The choice is presented to us by Paul: "So here's what I want you to do, God helping you: Take your everyday, ordinary life — your sleeping, eating, going-to-work, and *walking-around* life — and place it before God as an offering. Embracing what God does for you is the best thing you can do for him" (Romans 12:1, MSG, emphasis added).

Our guide in *choosing* the one thing is Mary of Bethany, who epitomizes what Oswald Chambers described when he wrote, "Christian sanctification is the indwelling holiness that guides our lives as spontaneously as its breathing. It depends not on my long-ings, yearning, praying, fasting, weeping, or howling, but entirely on my *will*."[2] Mary followed her heart, engaged her will, and found herself at the feet of Jesus — choosing the one thing.

Mary's Choice

Mary provides us with a picture of choosing that which, in Psalm 27, David so fervently desired: "to behold the beauty of the Lord" (verse 4). Is there any doubt that this psalm was one of Mary's favor-ites? David did his "beholding" in the house of the Lord, and Julian had her anchorhold. Mary's sanctuary of adoration was at the feet of Jesus. Every time she appears in the New Testament, we find her there.[3]

Read through this whole section, Luke 10:29-42, and notice how the gospel writer artfully illustrates with the Mary and Martha episode what it means to love God and with the Good Samaritan parable what it means to love your neighbor. Both stories have unlikely and unexpected heroes. In the parable, it was the despised

Samaritan who proved to be a neighbor rather than the "righteous" duo of priest and Levite. It is no less surprising for a woman in that patriarchal society to be extolled as the model disciple.

Jesus and His disciples were early in their circuitous journey to Jerusalem when they made a stop in Bethany at the house of Martha, evidently the oldest sibling and owner of the house. As the hostess in a culture where hospitality was not simply a value but an ethic, it was completely appropriate for Martha to be in the kitchen diligently preparing for her guests.

Completely inappropriate was the scene in the living room: Mary, a woman, taking the role of a student at the feet of a rabbi. It is true that the rabbis taught, "Let your house be a meetinghouse for the sages and sit amid the dust of their feet and drink in their words with thirst."[4] However, no proper rabbi would have permitted a woman that privilege, since they also taught that the words of the Torah should be burned before being handed over to a woman; that a wife should neither instruct children nor pray at the table; and that women were given to sensuality, witchcraft, and frivolity.[5] Jesus, with almost matter-of-fact kindness, subverts the misogynistic traditions by accepting and affirming Mary's choice of contemplation above catering.

Mary's bold decision[6] was a countercultural act of devotion. Though it may have seemed excessive to practical Martha, as Jonathan Edwards pointed out, "There is no such thing as excess in longings after the discoveries of the beauty of Christ Jesus."[7] We know from John 11 that Jesus loved Mary and Martha and their brother, Lazarus. Mary had seen firsthand the "beauty of Christ Jesus," and no prejudicial religious customs were going to keep her away from Him. We need her witness desperately today, for now, as then, "nothing is more opposed to true spirituality than conventional religion."[8]

Martha's Complaint

While Mary is seated and silent at Jesus' feet, Martha, the text tells us, is distracted, worried, and bothered in her preparations. Working alone, she gives outlet to her resentment by questioning Jesus: "Lord, do You not care . . . ?" (Luke 10:40). It matters little what follows those words. The wordless devotion of Mary is challenged by the wordy doubt of Martha.

Does Jesus prefer the ideal worker or the ideal worshiper?

On one occasion, as I meditated on this passage, I put myself in the place of Jesus to experience the event from His perspective. Mary's loving attention to my words was a stark contrast to Martha's worry and hurry. The surprising emotion that struck me was how hurtful it was that my friend Martha was too busy to listen to what I had to say. Jesus, like us in every way except sin, would not be immune to the human emotions surrounding this situation. His words reveal that, from His friends, He values devoted listening over distracted service.

Most of us, like Martha, have to learn this by experience. I certainly did. For some twelve years in active ministry, I was convinced that Jesus was a master who, more than anything, wanted my hard work. Like Martha, I became distracted by busyness, worried about outcomes, resentful toward people, and even angry at my Lord. All the while, Jesus was trying to send me a different message, but I wasn't listening. There was "eternal work" to be done, and I didn't have time for sitting at anyone's feet.

Since I refused to go to His feet, Jesus, in tender grace, came and washed mine (see John 13). To this day, sixteen years later, His intimate and strong words to me are still fresh: He said, "You work so hard for Me, but you have lost Me in the process. I am at work all over the world, and I will use you. Just love Me." I believe Jesus is speaking similar words wherever He finds "Martha Christianity" — duty without devotion, labor without love, productivity without peace. Jesus says to all those who are burning out, drying out, and running out, "I do not call you servants any longer, because the servant does not know what the master is doing; but I have called you friends, because I have made known to you everything that I have heard from my Father" (John 15:15, NRSV). My identity with Jesus had been as a servant, but He wanted me as a friend first. One of the sternest challenges to friendship with Jesus is doing work for Him. What is my work for Him if I don't know Him? Is it not an extension of my own ego in religious costume? Is it not a sprinkling of holy water on my goals, my plans, and my agendas? In my case, it was out-and-out idolatry. I was using Jesus as a means to the end of success in ministry. In the spirit of Martha, I considered God to be a simple condiment to add a little flavor to the meal that I was preparing. It was a choice that I made repeatedly, until I realized that what I do in work or ministry may or may not last (see 1 Corinthians 3:11-15), but what I do with Jesus becomes an eternal treasure for me.[9]

Jesus' Commendation

Martha was fuming about dinner; Mary was feasting on every word from the mouth of God (see Deuteronomy 8:3; Luke 4:4). Martha was troubled by many things; Mary chose the one thing. Martha was distracted; Mary was focused. Martha responded to Jesus in the light of the circumstances; Mary responded to the circumstances in the light of Jesus. Martha told Jesus what to do; Mary listened for what Jesus wanted her to do. Martha left Jesus to go to work; Mary left the work to go to Jesus. Martha initiated for Jesus; Mary responded to Jesus. Martha spoke to Jesus; Mary heard from Jesus. Martha was dutiful; Mary was devoted.

Because Mary *chose* to sit as a disciple, she received the

affirmation. Because she embraced the "one single duty" and chose "to gaze upon the master one has chosen and to listen,"[10] Jesus proclaimed that Mary had chosen the one thing necessary, the "good portion" (Luke 10:42, ESV), that would not be taken away from her. The psalmist declared the Lord to be his portion forever (see Psalm 73:25-26). Mary's "good portion" is the Lord Himself. That is why it can never be taken away.

Mary, like the old psalmists, chose to "set the LORD continually before me" (Psalm 16:8) because her heart knew that "the nearness of God is my good" (73:28). She chose the one thing, not because it was good for her — though it was — but because it was good. Friendship with Jesus *is* life, not something added in to make life better.

Rather than arguing about whether Jesus is *the* only way, maybe what is important is choosing Jesus as *my* only way, as Mary did. This means that I stop harboring secret ways of trying to make life work on my own and begin deciding in a thousand small ways every day to "learn Christ" (Ephesians 4:20). In so doing, I join Mary in "the inward habit of beholding God."[11]

Then we will understand the unanimous statement of the great cloud of witnesses who say, "When once you have seen Jesus, you can never be the same, other things do not appeal as they used to do."[12] This is the promise that Paul wrote of in 2 Corinthians 3:18: "But we all, with unveiled face, beholding as in a mirror the glory of the Lord, are being transformed into the same image from glory to glory, just as from the Lord, the Spirit." It is impossible to behold Jesus and not be transformed. Henri Nouwen sums it up beautifully:

Now do we see that the spiritual life in its utter simplicity is beholding Jesus? This may sound like an inviting call to a radically new way of living. What is new is that we have moved from the many things to the kingdom of God. What is new is that we are set free from the compulsions of our world and have set our hearts on the only necessary thing. What is new is that we no longer experience the many things, people, and events as endless causes for worry, but begin to experience them as the rich variety of ways in which God makes his presence known to us.[13]

We, along with Mary, have Jesus' commendation for our choice of the one thing. We also have His commendation for simply beholding Him. As Jesus told the disciples privately then, He commends us now: "Blessed are the eyes which see the things you see, for I say to you, that many prophets and kings wished to see the things which you see" (Luke 10:23-24), not to mention the angels who also "long to look" at what you and I have been given in Christ (see 1 Peter 1:12). I pray that the eyes of your heart will be enlightened that you may see the hope of His calling of you, the riches He has in you, and the power He has given you — all in Jesus who is all in all (see Ephesians 3:18-23).

CHAPTER 5

Søren Kierkegaard

The Life of Choosing the One Thing

> Whither should we turn, if not to Thee, Lord Jesus Christ? Where might the sufferer find consolation, if not in Thee? Ah, and where the penitent, if not with Thee, Lord Jesus Christ?
>
> — SØREN KIERKEGAARD

Søren Kierkegaard has appropriately been viewed as a poet, a prophet, a philosopher, and a theologian. However, his journals and spiritual writings reveal a man of prayer who, at his center, was struggling for his soul and seeking Jesus Christ.

Nowhere is this fact more clear than in his book *Purity of Heart Is to Will One Thing.* The title itself is an intriguing introduction into the life of choosing one thing. Eduard Geismar, who spent a lifetime studying Kierkegaard, wrote concerning this book, "It seems to me that nothing that he has written has sprung so directly out of his relationship with God as this address. Anyone who wishes to understand Kierkegaard properly will do well to begin with it."[1] So we will.

Who Was Søren Kierkegaard?

But before we do, let's briefly answer this question: Who was Søren Kierkegaard? The last of seven children, he was born in 1813 and lived nearly all of his life in Copenhagen, Denmark. Exempted by his father's wealth from the necessity of earning his own living, Søren was able to devote his adult life to study and writing. The simplicity of his outward story veils the complexity of his inward journey. His melancholy personality, which more than likely led to the breaking of his engagement to Regine Olsen, was best suited to a solitary life. Yet Søren was no recluse; he was seen frequently at the theater, on the streets of Copenhagen mingling with ordinary people, or in cafes with friends. He was a well-known figure in intellectual and religious circles, as well as in the broader community.

Søren's father, religiously pious and intellectually powerful, exerted a formative influence upon him. Young Kierkegaard's upbringing was characterized by his father's exhortation to him: "Be sure that you really love Jesus Christ."[2] Yet philosophically and experientially, conversion was a slow process for him. In his early twenties, he commented that if Christ were to come into his life, it would have to be through locked doors. The prodigal began his return in 1838, moving from a negative relationship to Christianity to an intellectual interest to a personal and inward identification to finally being a prophet for true faith in Christ.

Though Kierkegaard did not have "revelations" of the sort that Julian had, he nevertheless had at least three transformative experiences with God that set new directions in his life. For example, in 1847, he wrote what has become an oft-quoted line, "Now, with God's help, I shall be myself."[3] For him the forgiveness of sins was what freed him to be himself. Then, in 1851, he wrote, "I prayed to God that something new might be born within me. . . . Something new was born in me."[4] From that time on, he understood his vocation as a prophet for New Testament faith in a culture of watered-down religion. So now, let us listen to the words of the prophet.

That Solitary Individual

One day in July 2005, shepherds eating breakfast outside the town of Gevas, Turkey, were surprised to see a lone sheep jump off a nearby cliff and fall to its death. They were stunned, however, when the rest of the nearly 1,500 sheep in the herd followed, each leaping off the same cliff.[5]

Kierkegaard dedicated *Purity of Heart* to "that solitary individual." In doing so, he meant to cut each person from the herd. Separated from the crowd, the solitary individual is free to think and choose — free not to follow the crowd off the cliff. He wants to bring all of us face-to-face with our individual destiny, with our vocation, with the eternal, and with the God who has singled us out.

For Kierkegaard, choice, or the ability to "will one thing," springs from the inner core of the person. From this deep center, responsibility, remorse, and repentance also emerge. It is this center that can be dulled by the crowd, dissipated by busyness, and evaded through distractions and empty pleasures.

He sees these dangers clearly and, according to Douglas Steere,

> does not risk smothering his reader with leniency. He is prepared to be hard, to wound in order to heal, to use the knife. Kierkegaard conceived it his function as a writer to strip men of their disguises, to compel them to see evasions for what they are, to label blind alleys, to cut off men's retreats, . . . to enforce self-examination, and to bring them solitary and alone before the Eternal. Here he left them.[6]

He brings his readers to the place where they must choose. The escape hatches are closed. The safety nets have been removed. The excuses and delusions have been debunked. His readers stand exposed before the eternal God.

How does Kierkegaard bring us to that point? He reveals the subtle barriers to willing one thing. Then he shows us the price of willing one thing. Finally, he clarifies what must be done in order to will one thing.

Barriers to Willing One Thing

For Kierkegaard, only the eternal is always appropriate, always present, and always true. What a beautiful description of a living relationship to Jesus who "is the same yesterday and today and forever" (Hebrews 13:8). Slowly and methodically, Kierkegaard deconstructs the self-deceit that erects temporal barriers to willing the eternal one thing. His call is that of James 4:8: "Draw near to God and He will draw near to you. Cleanse your hands, you sinners; and purify your hearts, you double-minded."

These barriers are examples of the human tendency to double-mindedness and of the human resistance to willing one thing only. We want to keep our options open. Kierkegaard echoes Jesus, James, and a great cloud of witnesses who direct us to purify our hearts by choosing the one thing necessary.

Variety

A person could say that he wills one thing when he chooses pleasure. In reality, that person is willing a multitude of pleasures, not one thing. This is true of status, power, wealth, security, or any other temporal good. They only appear to be one thing, when they are actually many. As a result, the person becomes double-minded in will. Only the eternal is a unity, the one true thing.

Like us, Kierkegaard struggled with the many things and had difficulty submitting all of life to the one thing. He wrote, "The misfortune of my life is perhaps that I am interested in far too many things and not decidedly in some one thing; my interests are not all subordinated to one thing but are all co-ordinated."[7] It is worth noting that Kierkegaard considered the freedom to pursue a variety of interests as a "misfortune."

To place Jesus in the same lineup with anything else is to completely miss who He is and the nature of discipleship to Him. It would be comparable to a person choosing for his lunch among a rock, a nugget of iron ore, dirt, or a turkey sandwich. There is obviously only one real choice if a person wants to live. Is choosing Jesus that clear and simple for you?

A compromising self-delusion is the Jesus-and syndrome. When I am not ready to choose Jesus alone, it becomes convenient to choose one of His good gifts. It is so easy to tell ourselves that we are choosing Jesus when, in fact, we are choosing His peace, His guidance, or any number of His blessings. The test here is simple: Would I choose Jesus without His gifts of peace or guidance or anything else? Would I will Him and Him alone as my one thing? How do I respond to Jesus' bold invitation to follow Him? In that invitation there are no promises of happiness, peace, or success. There is only the promise of the presence of Jesus and life with Him.

Rewards

Similar to the barrier of variety is the barrier of rewards. Kierkegaard said that if I will the eternal for the sake of the reward, then I am willing two things, not one, and making myself double-minded. I am willing one thing only if I am not considering the reward.

The illustration he provides is the man who loves a woman because she has money. No one would call that man a lover. The true lover would love her despite her money, not because of it.

So the true lover of God is the one who loves God for God's sake, not for the rewards of being a God-lover. The existence of rewards — peace, joy, purpose, significance, health, success, blessings, and so forth — is of no concern. The lover of God can live with them or live without them. But many professing Christians seem to love the rewards more than the Rewarder, the gifts more than the Giver. These are the double-minded who have not yet willed one thing.

Fear of Punishment

Kierkegaard points out that willing the eternal out of fear of punishment is not willing one thing, but two, thus making this person double-minded as well. The underlying motive is avoidance of punishment, not relationship with God.

This kind of fear-based faith is a disheartening drama to watch, and, sadly, it is playing on many channels within Christianity. Filling our churches are good-hearted believers whose primary image of God is that of judge, referee, or demanding boss. Is it any wonder that, for so many, faith is a nervous performance in front of the squinty-eyed critic?

With that sort of vision, who can blame people for throwing themselves into working for God, while studiously avoiding any sort of intimacy with Him? They simply want to stay out of the Judge's line of fire. They want neither to draw near to God nor to have God draw near to them. Until they see God as the magnificent Lover revealed in Jesus, they will remain helplessly double-minded. Thinking they are choosing to serve God, they, by their avoidance of God, are actually choosing to serve their fears of God.

Ultimately, to overcome these barriers, I need to pray as Kierkegaard did:

> O Lord Jesus Christ, there is so much to drag us back: empty pursuit, trivial pleasures, unworthy cares. There is so much

*to frighten us away: a pride too cowardly to submit to being
helped, cowardly apprehensiveness which evades danger to its
own destruction, anguish for sin which shuns holy cleansing
as disease shuns medicine.
But Thou are stronger than these, so draw
Thou us now more strongly to Thee.*[8]

The Price of Willing One Thing

The price of willing one thing is microscopic compared to the tele-scopic glory of the life that it yields. Jesus perfectly describes this scenario in His parables of the hidden treasure and the pearl of great price (see Matthew 13:44-46). These parables portray the joyful exuberance of life in the kingdom of God—life that comes as a result of willing one thing.

Readiness to Be Exposed

Willing one thing requires that the individual is able to be himself or herself before God. We come to God just as we are, without pretense. Nowhere are facades and masks less useful than in the presence of a God who sees directly into hearts. We come naked, broken, wounded, confused, and sometimes rebellious into the waiting arms of the heavenly Father. From the place of love, I am free, just as I am, to will one thing.

Kierkegaard explained, "What is necessary is absolute trust, absolute openness, absolute sincerity. We should even ask God with all the sincerity that we possess that we might not falsely and unconsciously hide anything from him. The task is to become transparent before God in all our weakness and all our hope."[9]

Are you ready to be honest with God? Isn't it time to allow the gracious light of Christ to shine into the dark and locked closets of your soul? Can you risk standing naked in God's presence in order to be clothed with the righteousness of Christ?

If you answered yes, then you are ready to pray, "Arouse us, therefore, if we have dozed away into this delusion, save us from the error of wishing to admire Thee instead of being willing to follow Thee and to resemble Thee."[10]

Readiness to Suffer All

Comfortable, cozy Christianity was the order of the day in nineteenth-century Denmark, much as it is in twenty-first-century North America. In contrast, our Christian Scriptures were written out of the crucible of suffering. There is much talk about a "Christian worldview," but I have yet to hear expectation of suffering as part of the discussion. Yet for most followers of Jesus for most centuries, suffering was an expected reality, an acknowledged aspect of their worldview.

Kierkegaard observed, "Little by little, I noticed increasingly that all those whom God really loved . . . had to suffer in this world. Furthermore, that that is the teaching of Christianity: to be loved by God and to love God is to suffer."[11] Little more needs to be said in support of his observation than that we follow a crucified Lord.

To live in this fallen world is to experience pain — if not our own, then our neighbors'; if not our neighbors', then Jesus', as we fill up what is lacking in His suffering (see Colossians 1:24). So Kierkegaard rightly said, "The nearer to Thee, the more pain."[12] The closer we are to Jesus, the more His heart becomes our heart and His pain our pain over lost and broken people.

He also knew the reality of 1 Peter 4:13: "To the degree that you share the sufferings of Christ, keep on rejoicing, so that also at the revelation of His glory you may rejoice with exultation." So he wrote, "I know that in Thy love Thou sufferest with me more than I, Infinite Love."[13] Throughout Kierkegaard's *Journals*, suffering is not portrayed as a pain to be endured but as the way to joy. In the midst of the suffering, prayer is the consolation, the source of strength, and the means of transformation. As God worked in Kierkegaard through his prayers, joy emerged.

What, Then, Must I Do?

Having identified the barriers to and the price of pursuing the one thing, Kierkegaard turned his attention to the pursuit itself:

> What I really lack is to be clear in my mind *what I am to do*, not what I am to know, except in so far as a certain understanding must precede every action. The thing is to understand myself, to see what God really wishes *me* to do; the thing is to find a truth which is true *for me*, to find the *idea for which I can live and die*.[14]

That truth was Jesus. Kierkegaard wrote, "It is the imitation of Christ that must now be introduced and I must be what I am, in being different from others."[15] This imitation, much more than outward copying, is the radical inward transformation of one who has yielded in absolute self-surrender to God. For "only then can God shine through him so that he resembles God. However great he is, he cannot express this resemblance to God. God can only imprint Himself upon him when he himself has become nothing."[16]

Kierkegaard's ability to will one thing issued from the depth of his experience with God:

- "I have absolutely lived with God as one lives with a father. Amen."[17] This was the one "unshakeable thing" in his life.

- "He lets me weep before him in silent solitude, pour forth and again pour forth my pain, with the blessed consolation of knowing that he is concerned for me."[18]
- "It is wonderful how God's love overwhelms me."[19]
- "Through the unspeakable grace and help of God have I become myself."[20]

For Kierkegaard, the capstone of intimacy with God was losing one's own plans, agendas, and willfulness. This happened through earnest prayer where "the surprising thing happened to him. In proportion as he became more and more earnest in prayer, he had less and less to say, and in the end became quite silent."[21] We all begin by thinking that prayer is talking to God, but in time we realize that true prayer is to remain silent and listen to God.

Kierkegaard begins and ends *Purity of Heart* with the same prayer. I would encourage you to take some time to make this prayer your own:

Father in Heaven! What is a man without Thee! What is all that he knows, vast accumulation though it be, but a chipped fragment if he does not know Thee! What is all his striving, could it even encompass the world, but a half-finished work if he does not know Thee: Thee the One, who art one thing and who art all! So may Thou give to the intellect, wisdom to comprehend that one thing; to the heart, sincerity to receive this understanding; to the will, purity that wills only one thing. In prosperity may Thou grant perseverance to will one thing; amid distractions, collectedness to will one thing; in suffering, patience to will one thing.[22]

Jesus' Invitation to Choose the One Thing

"Come, follow Me."
— M A T T H E W   1 9 : 2 1

One will not, of course, turn away from what seems like the only game in town (political, economic, or religious) unless one has glimpsed a more attractive alternative. Jesus is a living parable, an audiovisual icon of that more attractive alternative.

— R I C H A R D   R O H R   A N D   J O H N   B O O K S E R   F E I S T E R

In C. S. Lewis's *The Silver Chair* (part of his CHRONICLES OF NARNIA series), Jill was dying of thirst, when she heard the rippling of a stream. As the clear, refreshing water came into view, so did Aslan, the huge lion and Christ figure. He was lying beside the stream as if guarding it. The intensity of Jill's thirst was matched only by her fear of the lion. At first she asked Aslan if he would go away while she drank. He refused. Then she asked him to promise not to hurt her. He said he made no such promises. She then concluded that she would find another stream, to which he replied, "There are no other streams."[1]

Jill had to choose. She wanted her thirst quenched on her own terms, only to discover that Aslan was not given to negotiation. Like Jill, we ask the Lord to step back so we can fill our thirsty souls with His blessings without dealing with Him. We want the living water Jesus offers as well as guarantees of protection from hurt and trouble. When Jesus declines to accommodate us, then we must choose. Will we look for other streams that are "lion-free" but whose waters are tepid and murky? Or will we risk all and choose to respond to Jesus' continual invitation, "Come to Me. . . . Learn from Me . . . and you will find rest for your souls" (Matthew 11:28-29)?

Our choice is the same as Jill's: remain safe, but thirsty, or respond to Jesus' amazing invitation to a life of rest and risk.

An Amazing Invitation

But what is the invitation I must respond to? There seem to be so many:

- Jesus said to the rich young ruler, who had kept the commandments and expressed interest in the kingdom of God, "Go and sell your possessions and give to the poor . . . and come, follow Me" (Matthew 19:21).
- He said to the woman caught breaking the commandment against adultery, "Neither do I condemn you; go and sin no more" (John 8:11, NKJV).
- Jesus proclaimed to the righteous Nicodemus, "You must be born again" (John 3:7).
- To the immoral woman at the well, He said, "Whoever drinks of the water that I will give him shall never thirst; but the water that I will give him will become in him a well of water springing up to eternal life" (John 4:14).
- He instructed believing Jews to abide in His word to prove they were His disciples: "If you continue in My word, then you are truly disciples of Mine" (John 8:31).
- To the Twelve the night before He died, Jesus said, "If you love Me, you will keep My commandments" (John 14:15).
- Of Mary of Bethany, who was simply sitting at His feet listening, He said, "Only one thing is necessary, for Mary has chosen the good part" (Luke 10:42).

Which is it, Jesus? Is it selling all and following You or sitting in my house listening at Your feet? Is it obeying Your commands or experiencing forgiveness when I don't? Is it searching the Scriptures or not? What does it mean to follow You, Jesus? What am I supposed to do? What are the steps? What is the key? Isn't there a secret? Should I pray like Jabez? Maybe a life driven by purpose is the answer. It seems so hard, so complicated. It seems like everyone else gets it and I don't. Everyone else is so sure of themselves and I'm not. It makes me tired and wears me out.

What is that to you? You follow Me.

What was that, Lord? What did You say? Just follow You? It is that simple? But how?

In Matthew 11, Jesus answers my cry,

Are you tired? Worn out? Burned out on religion? Come to me. Get away with me and you'll recover your life. I'll show you how to take a real rest. Walk with me and work with me — watch how I do it. Learn the unforced rhythms of grace. I won't lay anything heavy or ill-fitting on you. Keep company with me and you'll learn to live freely and lightly. (11:28-30, MSG)

That's what I want! That's it — being with You and learning from You how to live my life. Wow! No formulas or recipes or gimmicks — just following my Leader and Teacher into all of life — work, play, family, friendships, worship, prayer, study, and service.

He reassures me, *I came that you might have life, and have it excessively* (John 10:10, PAR).

Jesus, it's amazing that You want for me what I want for myself — life to the full, life to the extreme, the best life possible.

This is the life of learning the "unforced rhythms of grace" by following Jesus into His way, His truth, and His life. In so doing, I experience "the kingdom within" — a life that is gracful, unforced, and rhythmic. A life that is "athirst and empty, for God's breath to fill."[2]

There is one choice that I must make in order to enter this life: Who is going to lead my life? That choice is between two masters — Jesus or me. Am I going to continue to be the master of my own destiny, to be the leader of my life, and the ruler of my own kingdom? Or, am I ready to give up the project of running my own life and admit that I need a new Master, Leader, and Teacher? This is what it means to become a disciple, an apprentice of Jesus. Rather than a badge of honor, choosing to become a disciple is a humble admission of incompetence. This is what it means to choose Jesus above all else.

Dallas Willard drives home the absolute necessity of our choosing to become a disciple:

> But the final step in becoming a disciple is decision. We become a life student of Jesus by deciding. When we have achieved clarity on "the costs" — on what is gained and what is lost by becoming or failing to become his apprentice — an effective decision is then possible. But still it must be made. It will not just happen. We do not drift into discipleship.[3]

This is the "one thing necessary" that Mary chose and the one thing that Kierkegaard willed.

Choosing a Graced Life

How is it that the promised life of rest can look more like anxious striving? How has the simple act of coming to Jesus and learning from Him been made to appear complicated and out of reach for the ordinary disciple? Could it be that our activist, self-help culture has diluted the vision of a graced life and even corrupted the path itself, the spiritual disciplines?

Ways of Receiving

First and foremost, spiritual disciplines are "means of grace" — ways of receiving something from God, not doing something for Him. They work on us, not on God. They are ways of accessing the infinite resources of the kingdom of God for our lives. If you have an ATM card, you understand how this works. You could have thousands of dollars in your bank account, but if you don't have a card and a personal identification number, you don't have access to what is rightfully yours.

The spiritual disciplines provide access to the abundant life. When Jesus spent forty days in the desert, fasting in solitude before facing the tempter, He was receiving strength for the battle ahead — accessing resources from the Father. So, as His apprentices, we follow Jesus into His practices to gain, as He did, the power to face the challenges and trials of life.

Many of us have grown up with the idea that because of God's grace, there is nothing for us to do except be acted upon. This sort of passive "quietism" was declared a heresy a few centuries ago. Grace is God working *with* me to accomplish what I couldn't through natural human effort alone. It does not eliminate the need for human striving. The life of grace is the easy yoke, but it is still a yoke. I show up and I participate — and sometimes that participation requires the very best of my energy and intelligence.

Broccoli or Brownie

I eat broccoli because it's good for me (and my wife makes me). I eat a brownie because it's *good*! When you think of spiritual disciplines, are you thinking broccoli or brownies? Once we make the connection that an intentional life of following Jesus is not just good for us but really good — the best life possible, in fact — we have "brownie" motivation. The disciplines are warm, rich brownies for the soul. How might it change your approach to life if your thought was, *I get to connect with God through the spiritual disciplines*, instead of, *I have to practice the disciplines?*

Disciplines, Not Discipline

In Matthew 11:29-30, Jesus described the life of following Him with the words, "My yoke is easy." There is a dual word picture here. The immediate image is that of a stronger, older ox yoked with a smaller, younger ox. All the smaller ox must do to feel his burden lessen is to walk in step alongside his more competent partner. For us, the disciplines are ways to help us "keep in step" with Jesus, "casting all [our] care upon Him" (1 Peter 5:7, NKJV), so that He is pulling the weight of life for us. They keep our life in rhythm with Jesus'. Living this way is far easier and lighter than carrying the burdens of life myself — it is the easy yoke.

The other, more subtle word picture comes from the world of the Jewish rabbi, whose set of interpretations of the Torah, God's loving instruction to His people, was called his "yoke."[4] These rabbis had elaborate and detailed prescriptions of how to live according to the Torah, all of which required strict discipline. Jesus came along and proclaimed that His yoke is easy because He reduced the hundreds of complex commandments that compose the Torah to the simplicity of loving God and loving neighbor. It is also easy because, as He teaches in the Sermon on the Mount, obedience flows from the inside out (see Matthew 5:1–6:29). The inner transformation produced by the spiritual disciplines frees me to become inwardly the kind of person who loves God and others outwardly. As Dallas Willard said, "The disciplines for the spiritual life are available, concrete activities designed to render bodily beings such as we ever more sensitive and receptive to the Kingdom of Heaven brought to us in Christ, even while living in a world set against God."[5]

For example, I cannot through my will alone simply decide to love my irritating coworker, when my heart is filled with anger toward her. However, through the spiritual discipline of praying the psalms, I can learn to pray my anger, as the psalmists do, freeing me to love those who previously angered me. Rather than trying harder through discipline to be more patient with my children, I can enter into the spiritual discipline of silence for ten minutes a day and allow the inner peace created to flow into my relationship with my children.

Choosing an Unforced Life

Immediately after young David had accepted the challenge to fight Goliath, Saul forced his armor upon David, thinking that what had worked for him as king would work for David. It didn't. David could barely walk in the ill-fitting armor, so he discarded it for what was congenial to his experience, strengths, and current situation — five smooth stones and a sling (see 1 Samuel 17:38-39). David's tools would have been of no use to Saul or the other soldiers, just as their armor was of no use to David. Forcing someone else's armor on myself doesn't work in military battle, nor does it work in the spiritual battle. Yet many followers of Christ seem to be trying to wear their pastor's armor, or armor from a book they have read, or the armor of a ministry they have served. As a result, like David, they can hardly walk and stumble repeatedly in the life of faith.

It Is About You!

Contrary to what I may initially think, my relationship with Jesus has to be tailored to the unique creation of God that I am. Do you remember how, as we observed in the beginning of this chapter, Jesus responded so differently to each individual? That is because each one had a unique personality and background, as well as unique needs. If the infinite Creator God chose to create each human being as His workmanship, literally His "poem" (*workmanship*, in Ephesians 2:10, comes from the Greek word *poiema*), don't you think His ongoing work of blessing and saving that person would be beautifully crafted for each individual? This means that my response to the creating and saving God is original and creative work. It is creative in the sense that I am responding to God out of the materials of *my* life, much as an artist creates using paints, musical notes, or words. Cooperating with my Creator and Redeemer, I become the artist of my own life.

Some five hundred years ago, Francis de Sales reflected an ancient wisdom when he wrote, "Devotion must be exercised in different ways by the gentleman, the worker, the servant, the prince, the widow, the young girl, and the married woman. Not only is this true, but the practice of devotion must also be adapted to the strength, activities, and duties of each particular person."[6] As Paul wrote in Galatians 5:1, "It was for freedom that Christ set us free" — freedom to develop a personal and intimate relationship with God in the real and ordinary circumstances that are our lives. This is not out of reach for any of us.

Pray as You Can, Not as You Can't

As obvious as this sounds, it is surprising how often in prayer sincere disciples impose on themselves ways of praying that are as ill-fitting as a big sister's dress. Rather than hand-me-down prayers, we have been given a custom-tailored wardrobe of conversation with God. The Cistercian monk Andre Louf explains,

> Authentic prayer can never be learnt from someone else.
> It has its own instructor within it. Prayer is God's gift to

[the one] who prays. . . . Thus prayer is the precious fruit of the Word — Word of God that has become wholly our own and in that way has been inscribed deep in our body and our psyche, and that now can become our response to the love of the Father. The Spirit stammers it out in our heart, without our doing anything about it. It bubbles up, it flows, it runs like living water.[7]

When you are struggling with prayer, you might try this assignment: For as long as you can, don't pray. When you realize that you can't *not* pray, what sort of prayer arises within you? What "bubbles up" is the kind of prayer that is most you. Start there, be attentive to the unique gift of prayer given you, and pray as you can.

Choosing a Rhythmic Life

My first encounter with the world of spiritual disciplines was over twenty years ago when I first read Richard Foster's wonderful book *The Celebration of Discipline*. I loved it, but I saw little hope of integrating what I had read into a life already full with a young family and a demanding ministry. It seemed to be an all-or-nothing proposition — a disciplined life with Christ or the conventional life of hurry and flurry. What escaped me was the possibility of a *via media,* a middle way between the two opposites. Walking the middle way means learning from Jesus how to live in God's rhythms of work and Sabbath, feasting and fasting, community and solitude, service and study, interaction and silence.

Learn from Jesus

To be a disciple is to be the student or apprentice of a master. Jesus is the master of life, the expert on the kind of life that glorifies the

Father, that loves and serves others, and that produces personal transformation. Here are some suggestions for learning from Jesus how to live in His kingdom through the practice of the spiritual disciplines:

- Take seriously your situation in life and choose a few disciplines accordingly. The commuter could use drive time as a sanctuary on wheels to worship, to listen to, or to be still before the Lord.
- Identify those times when you profoundly experience God's presence. Place intentionality and commitment around them. If it is through the beauty of God's creation, then plan to take a walk with Jesus on an outdoor trail twice a week.
- Don't be afraid to experiment with a variety of practices. Incorporate those that are helpful and discard the ones that aren't. For example, it is easy to get in a rut with Bible reading. Perhaps read through the entire Bible one year, but the next year, *slowly* read and meditate on one book each month.
- Add and delete disciplines as needed as your life changes. Be aware of the seasons and rhythms of this creative relationship with the God who loves us. The mother of young children may not have the option of enjoying extended times of solitude, but she can practice the presence of God in the midst of dirty diapers and carpooling.[8]

The Magnetic Attraction of Holiness

Choosing Jesus above all others, I follow my Master into His practices of communion with the Father. As I do, my life begins to have that same powerful attraction that His did. In a world of anger and hate, a life of love stops people in their tracks. For the anxious and restless, a life filled with the peace of God is irresistible.

This is why the multitudes were drawn to Jesus.

This is why thousands went to the wilderness of Egypt to find Anthony, the earliest of the desert fathers, and to share the fruit of his solitude and silence.

Centuries later, it is why journalists, TV cameras, indeed, the whole world beat a path to the door of the diminutive Albanian nun in Calcutta, Mother Teresa.

This is why you, right where you are, can be as Jesus said, "the light of the world" (Matthew 5:14) and "the salt of the earth" (5:13) simply by living "the unforced rhythms of grace" (11:29, MSG).

In so doing, you will have *chosen* the one true thing.

A closing prayer for our continued choosing of the one thing necessary:

I need thee to teach me day by day, according to each day's opportunities and needs. Give me, O my Lord, that purity of conscience which alone can receive, which alone can improve thy inspiration. My ears are dull, so that I cannot hear thy voice. My eyes are dim, so that I cannot see thy tokens. Thou alone canst quicken my hearing, and purge my sight, and cleanse and renew my heart. Teach me to sit at thy feet and to hear thy Word, Amen.[9]

valuing

the

one

thing

A Glorious Ambition

I count all things to be loss in view of the surpassing *value* of knowing Christ. . . . I do not regard myself as having laid hold of it yet; but *one thing* I do: . . . I press on toward the goal for the prize of the upward call of God in Christ Jesus.

— PHILIPPIANS 3:8,13-14 (EMPHASIS ADDED)

If you continue to love Jesus, nothing much can go wrong with you, and I hope you may always do so.

— C. S. LEWIS

CHAPTER 7

Philippians 3

Valuing the One Thing over the Many

A day in Your courts is better than a thousand outside.
I would rather stand at the threshold of the house of my God
Than dwell in the tents of wickedness.
— PSALM 84:10

A saint is one who exaggerates what the world neglects.
— G. K. CHESTERTON

I was a freshman in college when I first saw the value of knowing Jesus. One of the experiences that formed me was singing the song "He's Everything to Me" by Ralph Carmichael. Practically every time the group I was a part of gathered, we would sing that song. It called forth from me an expression of devotion and a sense of value far beyond that of the reading, teaching, or preaching to which I was exposed. That song gave me my first taste of the "allness" and "everythingness" of Jesus Christ — a glimpse of valuing one thing over the many.

Though we can talk about them separately, desires, choices, and values are inextricably bound together. For example, the above-mentioned college experience was a result of some wise choices that grew out of a desire for something more in life. The result was a change in what I valued. That is the normal pattern of growth and transformation. But it is certainly not a mechanical, linear process.

Desires lead us to choices. Choices repetitively made in a certain direction congeal into values. Our values are what they are as a result of our desires and choices — who we are. As I direct my desires and choices, over time my values change. Hence, the movement of this book has been from desiring to choosing to valuing. Always and in everything, the Holy Spirit is initiating, guiding, teaching, empowering, and directing the movements of our journeys.

Counting All Things Loss

Martha was preoccupied with many things and had not learned to count these things as loss. Her value system was crowded, as was her heart. As a result, she became worried, bothered, and resentful — the fruit of her busyness. The joy of valuing the one thing necessary is a life of simplicity, unity, and freedom; a life like Mary's; a life of sitting at Jesus' feet.

Résumé

The apostle Paul provides for us another picture of valuing the one thing. It comes from his own story as told in Philippians 3:4-16. In the first few verses, he gives his résumé: circumcised, of the tribe of Benjamin, Hebrew of Hebrews, zealous, and a blameless Pharisee. Paul was a religious superman. That is why he says that he has far more reason to put confidence in natural human ability (flesh) than anyone.

All of these credentials would have been looked upon as assets in his first-century world. Yet Paul says and does the unimaginable. He takes all that he has going for him as a faithful Jew, his lifelong work, and transfers it from the asset column to the liability column. In essence, he becomes spiritually and religiously bankrupt.

He goes even further, this radical Paul, and counts *all things* loss. I would guess this means his assets as a person, a Roman citizen, and an intellectual, as well as whatever material goods he may have possessed.

Rubbish

To put an exclamation point on this massive transfer, Paul states that he counts all of this "stuff" he has let go of as *skybalon*. This depressing Greek word means "rubbish and muck of many kinds: excrement, rotten food, bits left at a meal as not worth eating, a rotting corpse. Nastiness and decay are the constant elements of its meaning; it is a coarse, ugly, violent word implying worthlessness, uselessness, and repulsiveness."[1] There is not a stronger word that he could have used.

Reasons

Why would Paul divest himself of every earthly asset and then call them garbage? He gives one strong but simple reason: *"the surpassing value of knowing Christ Jesus"* (Philippians 3:8, emphasis added).

He knew that Jesus was either everything or He was nothing.

He knew, in the words of a psalm he had prayed many times, that "a day in Your courts is better than a thousand outside" (Psalm 84:10).

He knew, in the words he himself wrote in 2 Corinthians 4:7, that those many things were only "earthen vessels" and that Jesus was the "treasure" of incalculable value. Paul defied the insane human tendency to venerate the vessel and neglect the treasure.

Can you imagine how silly it would be to receive as a gift a priceless masterpiece, only to hang the box on the wall instead of the painting? As ludicrous as it is to value the box over the masterpiece that came in it, it is even more so to value any "earthen vessel" above the Jesus treasure that it contains.

This reflection on Philippians 3 sends my mind back ten years to our daughter Keely's senior year in high school. She was very active in extracurricular activities and earned her share of awards. Instead of listing all of those activities and awards by her picture in the high school annual, as most of the seniors did, she chose to do something that more accurately reflected her values. Next to her picture were these words: "I count all things to be loss in view of the surpassing value of knowing Christ Jesus my Lord" (Philippians 3:8).

The Surpassing Value

Philippians 3 is not the only place where Paul articulates the value of the one true thing. He makes another clear value comparison in Romans 8:18: "For I consider that the sufferings of this present time are not worthy to be compared with the glory that is to be revealed to us." In Philippians 3, what is gained through knowing Jesus is exponentially greater than anything that is lost. In other words, there is no cost — just an incredible bargain. In Romans 8, the value of the eternal glory of knowing Jesus makes any present suffering seem light and momentary (see also 2 Corinthians 4:17).

The life of David Livingstone is a marvelous example of this surpassing value even in the midst of suffering. Livingstone wrote,

> People talk of the sacrifice I have made in spending so much of my life in Africa. . . . Anxiety, sickness, suffering, or danger, now and then, with a foregoing of the common conveniences of this life, may make us pause, and cause the spirit to waver, and the soul to sink; but let this be only for a moment. All these are nothing when compared with the glory which shall hereafter be revealed in, and for, us. I never made a sacrifice.[2]

"I never made a sacrifice" — what an incredible witness to the reality of the glory! Livingstone truly reflected Jesus, who said, "My food is to do the will of Him who sent Me" (John 4:34).

Treasure

Livingstone was among those, like Paul, who understood the difference between the treasure and the vessel. Suffering impacts us at the level of vessel. If my focus is constantly on the treasure, knowing Jesus, then I can say along with Paul, "We do not lose heart, but though our outer man is decaying, yet our inner man is being renewed day by day" (2 Corinthians 4:16).

Is Jesus my treasure? The best way to answer that question is to ask another. Do I value Jesus as my source of wisdom and strength for every aspect of my life? Or, as Dallas Willard frames the issue,

> Strangely, we seem prepared to learn how to live from almost anyone but him. . . . Where we spontaneously look for "information" on how to live shows how we truly feel and who we really have confidence in. And nothing more forcibly demonstrates the extent to which we automatically assume the irrelevance of Jesus as teacher for our "real" lives.[3]

And nothing more forcibly demonstrates that I treasure Jesus as my one true thing.

Truth

How then do I begin to embrace Jesus as my treasure and to value Him above all else? It is a matter, as Dallas Willard pointed out, of whom I put my confidence in, of whom I trust, of where my faith is. And that faith comes through hearing the Word concerning Christ (see Romans 10:17). The "hearing" that generates faith is far more than listening with the mind; it is listening with the heart. As Jonathan Edwards, who was likely the greatest theologian America has produced, wrote,

> There are thousands who hear the Word of God, who hear great and exceedingly important truths about themselves and their lives, and yet all they hear has no effect upon them, makes no change in the way they live. The reason is this: they are not affected with what they hear. . . . I am bold in saying this, but I believe that no one is ever changed, either by doctrine, by hearing the Word, or by the preaching or teaching of another, unless the affections are moved by these things. No one ever seeks salvation, no one ever cries for wisdom, no one ever wrestles with God, no one ever kneels in prayer or flees from sin, with a heart that remains unaffected. In a word, there is never any great achievement by the things of religion without a heart deeply affected by those things.[4]

Even as you read these pages, have you found yourself crying for wisdom, wrestling with God, or kneeling in prayer? If your heart has not been deeply affected, then we have both failed.

If that is the case, then there is even greater urgency to understand that the truth is Jesus. As Paul honestly and humbly confessed, "I determined to know nothing among you except Jesus Christ, and Him crucified" (1 Corinthians 2:2). Such radical exclusiveness eliminated for Paul even good things such as human wisdom, clever speech, and persuasive personality — the very vessels we are so tempted to value above the treasure. Therefore we would be wise to "turn a deaf ear to anyone who preaches to you without speaking of Jesus Christ."[5]

That counsel is part of the wisdom of the Christian spiritual tradition that is also reflected by Philip Jacob Spener:

> It is certain that a young man who fervently loves God, although adorned with limited gifts, will be more useful to the church of God with his limited meager talent and academic achievement than a vain and worldly fool with double doctor's degrees who is very clever but has not been taught by God. The work of the former is blessed, and he is aided by the Holy Spirit. The latter has only a carnal knowledge, with which he can easily do more harm than good.[6]

Jesus is the truth and the treasure — the one true value for living.

Training

We can't simply decide to value Jesus above all else, but we can train toward that way of being. Paul, at the end of Philippians 3, emphasizes this path when he says, "But one thing I do: . . . I press on toward the goal for the prize of the upward call of God in Christ Jesus" (verses 13-14). This "pressing" sounds strenuous, similar to athletic training toward a goal. Here are some encouragements for your own pressing toward valuing the one thing:

- *Know Christ* before working for Christ. As Oswald Chambers perceptively wrote, "We slander God by our very eagerness to work for God without knowing Him."[7]
- *Live Christ* before winning others to Christ. John Oxenham asked, "Would you win the world for Christ? One way there is and only one: you must live Christ from day to day and see His will be done."[8]

- *Learn Christ*, not the ways of the world. In Paul's words, "You did not learn Christ in this way, if indeed you have heard Him and have been taught in Him, just as truth is in Jesus" (Ephesians 4:20-21).
- *Adore Christ* more than accomplishment. When the woman at the home of Simon the leper anointed Jesus with a bottle of costly perfume, some grumbled at the waste. But Jesus rebuked them, saying, "She has done a beautiful thing *to* me" (Mark 14:6, ESV, emphasis added).

In each of these actions, we do as Augustine suggests: "Sing but keep on walking."[9] Walking is pressing on in the ordinary routine of life toward the goal of being with and being like Jesus — this "one thing I do." Singing reflects the joy that inevitably comes to those who value the one thing above the many things.

CHAPTER 8

Ignatius of Loyola

The Life of Valuing the One Thing

When we are called to follow Christ, we are summoned to an exclusive attachment to his person.
— DIETRICH BONHOEFFER

The following prayer, "Soul of Christ," appears at the beginning of Ignatius of Loyola's book of spiritual exercises. One of his favorite prayers, it serves as an introduction to his fervent, Christ-centered spirituality:

Jesus, may all that is you flow into me.
May your body and blood be my food and drink.
May your passion and death be my strength and life.
Jesus, with you by my side enough has been given.
May the shelter I seek be the shadow of your cross.
Let me not run from the love which you offer,
But hold me safe from the forces of evil.
On each of my dyings shed your light and your love.
Keep calling to me until that day comes,
When, with your saints, I may praise you forever. Amen.[1]

Pray it again. Slow down. Reflect. Pause. Listen to the Spirit within you. How is the Spirit speaking into your life through this prayer?

Who Was Ignatius of Loyola?

Ignatius of Loyola was born into a noble Basque family in 1491. A young man with a fiery temper, he trained in the household of the High Treasurer for Ferdinand and Isabella to be a courtier/knight. He was preoccupied with visions of chivalry and heroism.

At age twenty-six, he was badly injured in a battle with the French at Pamplona in Spain when a cannonball crushed one leg. Moved to his family castle in northern Spain, he underwent two excruciating operations to repair his shattered leg. He endured the second surgery so that he could walk without a limp and dance, enabling him to resume his life of romance and chivalry.

During the long convalescence, he found himself daydreaming in two distinct directions. In the first, he dreamed of a life as a noble knight performing heroic acts of courage, and in the second, of a life of following Christ in hardship and imitation of the saints. Having asked for books about the exploits of the knights, he was given instead *Vita Christi* (*Life of Christ*) by Ludolph of Saxony and the *Golden Legend* (a collection of the lives of the saints) by Jacobus de Voragine to read during his recovery.

As he reflected and wrote on his reading and daydreaming, he noticed that his worldly fantasies left him dry and discontent, but his thoughts of Jesus and the saints made him satisfied and joyful. In this way, God used his imagination to draw him to faith, and in 1521, the same year that Luther was excommunicated, Ignatius was converted to Christ.[2]

For Ignatius, as for many others, the initial coming to Christ was an exercise in valuing the one thing over all others. He concluded that the value of following Jesus, even in hardship, was far greater than that of worldly happiness and accomplishment. This was similar to what the writer of Hebrews said of Moses' valuing of the one thing:

By faith Moses, when he had grown up, refused to be called the son of Pharaoh's daughter, choosing rather to endure ill-treatment with the people of God than to enjoy the passing pleasures of sin, considering the reproach of Christ greater riches than the treasures of Egypt; for he was looking to the reward. (Hebrews 11:24-26)

In this case, Moses' sense of the value of relationship with God led to the sacrificial choice of the "reproach of Christ" over the "treasures of Egypt." He knew he had a better treasure.

The Spiritual Exercises

Ignatius came to faith by means of a Spirit-prompted imagination. That, along with an acute awareness of his own inner experience, led him to develop an intense desire for intimacy with Christ. "For," Ignatius wrote, "it is not knowing much, but realizing and relishing things interiorly, that contents and satisfies the soul."[3] This desire was deepened by the lifelong impact that Thomas à Kempis's book *The Imitation of Christ*[4] had upon him. He came to value knowing and following Jesus above everything.

The Society of Jesus

What Ignatius learned about his own interior development, he passed on to his friends. His personal notes of his own journey with Christ evolved into *The Spiritual Exercises* as he used them in ministry with others. In 1534 they called themselves simply, "friends in the Lord." By 1540 Ignatius and his ten companions were officially recognized as a missionary order, the Society of Jesus.

The initial draft of the order's constitution included this paragraph describing the character of those who would belong:

He is a member of a community founded chiefly to strive for the progress of souls in Christian life and doctrine, and for the propagation of the faith by means of the ministry of the word, the Spiritual Exercises, and works of charity, and specifically by the instruction of children and unlettered persons in Christianity.[5]

This brief statement captures much of what would become the "charism," or special gifting, of the Jesuits for the next five centuries. If one didn't know differently, it very well could have been the mission statement for any number of Protestant evangelical missionary organizations.

During Ignatius's lifetime, most of the Jesuits' work was directed toward the spiritual welfare of individuals and small groups. The ministry to individuals occurred through the offering of spiritual direction and exercises, while teaching and preaching were offered in small group settings. Members of the Society also engaged in foreign missionary work in India and Brazil. These kinds of ministries by the Society of Jesus continue to this day.

Experiencing the Exercises

My friendship with Ignatius began in 1991. At that time, I was guided through his *Spiritual Exercises* by a Jesuit spiritual director. The exercises have been a powerful tool for deep transformation for almost five hundred years, and they certainly were for me. They are a way of praying through and experiencing the life of Jesus in a direct and personal way. Though the exercises immerse you in Scripture, they are an experience of deep conversion by the Spirit's formative work more than they are a Bible study.

The various exercises engage the imagination, senses, mind, body, and heart — the whole person — in powerful ways. The purpose is to lead a person into true spiritual freedom, and it is attained by "bringing an order of *values* into our lives so that we make no choice or decisions" that would detract from our walk with Jesus.[6] They teach us how to value the one thing.

The exercises begin with what Ignatius called "The Principle and Foundation." It is both an introduction to and summary of the exercises, so I want to identify a few highlights from it:

- "God freely created us so that we might know, love, and serve Him in this life and be happy with Him forever."[7] Here is God's vision for our lives, God's purpose for us. Ignatius declared that the only purpose of life is to know Jesus Christ better. All that follows in the exercises is rooted in this foundational vision.

- "All the things in this world are gifts of God, created for us, to be the means by which we can come to know Him better, love Him more surely, and serve Him more faithfully."[8] Everything that God created was designed to help us live out the purpose for which we were created. God is the Creator and Giver of every good gift (see James 1:17) and, as our loving Father, delights in giving us what we need (see Matthew 7:7-11).

- "As a result, we ought to appreciate and use these gifts of God insofar as they help us toward our goal of loving service and union with God."[9] Now Ignatius is helping us to see from the perspective of the one thing. All created gifts funnel down to the one purpose for which we were created: loving relationship with God.

- "But insofar as any created things hinder our progress toward our goal, we ought to let them go."[10] This is where our desires and choices can be governed by Spirit-led discernment. Ignatius does not legislate. There is no coercive force or subtle manipulation. He simply offers guidance concerning how we can freely decide what we need to let go.

- "In everyday life, then, we should keep ourselves indifferent or undecided in the face of all created gifts when we have an option and we do not have the clarity of what would be a better choice. We ought not to be led on by our natural likes and dislikes even in matters such as health or sickness, wealth or poverty, between living in the east or in the west, becoming an accountant or a lawyer."[11] This is radical and biblical guidance that one seldom hears in twenty-first-century America. On a retreat, I heard one spiritual director refer to this as "passionate indifference to anything but Christ." What a great statement! What a wonderful way to think about valuing the one thing! To be passionate for Christ, the one true thing, is to be passionately indifferent to the many things. This concept is inherent in Paul's statement that he had "learned to be content in whatever circumstances" (Philippians 4:11) and he had "learned the secret of being filled and going hungry, both of having abundance and suffering need" (4:12). It must be a secret because there are so few who even attempt it. But Paul and Ignatius are trying to set us free from this enslaving compulsion to have our own way, to get what we want when we want it, and to be safe, comfortable, and healthy. It is actually possible to be passionately indifferent to all of those.

- "Rather, our only desire and our one choice should be that option which better leads us to the goal for which God created us."[12] Ignatius clarifies for us why it is possible to count all things loss for the surpassing value of knowing Christ. If I have *one desire* and *one choice*, then the goal for which I have been created has captivated me and I am valuing that one thing. And life becomes beautifully simple. I have a fulcrum on which every decision, option, activity, and desire can turn. It is simply this question: Which decision would enable me to know and love Jesus more faithfully?

Why They Work So Well

The exercises of Ignatius have been around for 450 years because they are an incredibly congenial vessel in which to carry devotion to Jesus Christ. They draw upon the text of Scripture in order to work on the text of our lives. They provide exactly what Eugene Peterson wrote that we need:

> It is a matter of urgency that interest in our souls be matched by an interest in our Scriptures — and for the same reason: they, the Scripture and souls, are the primary fields of operation of the Holy Spirit. An interest in souls divorced from an interest in Scripture leaves us without a text that shapes these souls. In the same way, an interest in Scripture divorced from an interest in souls leaves us without any material for the text to work on.[13]

The exercises become that matrix in which our souls and Scripture can play.

The approach to Scripture that is learned in the exercises precludes us from falling victim to the huge and deadly blunder of the Pharisees, to whom Jesus said, "You search the Scriptures because you think that in them you have eternal life; it is these that testify about Me; and you are unwilling to come to Me so that you may have life" (John 5:39-40). Pharisees, then and now, use Scripture for their own purposes rather than receiving it for transformation.

In this sense, Scripture is like art, as C. S. Lewis explains,

When we "receive" it we exert our senses and imagination and various other powers according to a pattern invented by the artist. When we "use" it we treat it as assistance for our own activities. . . . "Using" is inferior to "reception" because art, if used rather than received, merely facilitates, brightens, relieves or palliates our life, and does not add to it.[14]

When I "receive" the written Word of God, it is impossible to miss the Living Word. In so doing, I move into the purpose for which I have been created — to know and love the God of the Word.

Yet Jesus said there is hope even for scribes and Pharisees: "Therefore every scribe who has become a disciple of the kingdom of heaven is like a head of a household, who brings out of his treasure things new and old" (Matthew 13:52). Remember the purpose of the exercises — conversion. It is possible even for a scribe to choose to become a disciple of the kingdom. When he does, he experiences the joy of an inner treasure, out of which he lives and loves. The "old things" represent the ancient Word of God within him. The "new things" represent the personalizing of the old truths in a new time and a new place within the disciple. This is what Paul envisioned when he wrote, "Let the word of Christ richly dwell within you" (Colossians 3:16).

So indeed, we do have a treasure in an earthen vessel when we learn the life of valuing the one thing above all else. Thomas Kelly describes what this life looks like in full flower:

There is a way of life so hid with Christ in God that in the midst of the day's business one is inwardly lifting brief prayers, short [bursts] of praise, subdued whispers of adoration and of tender love to the Beyond that is within. One can live in a well-nigh continuous state of unworded prayer, directed toward God, directed toward people and enterprises we have on our heart. There is no hurry about it at all; it is a life unspeakable and full of glory, an inner world of splendor within which we, unworthy, may live. Some of you know it and live in it; others of you may wistfully long for it; it can be yours. Now out from such a holy Center come the commissions of life. Our fellowship with God issues in world concern. We cannot keep the love of God to ourselves.[15]

CHAPTER 9

Jesus' Invitation to Value the One Thing

"Whoever does not carry the cross
and follow me cannot be my disciple."
— LUKE 14:27 (NRSV)

Christianity without discipleship is always Christianity without Christ.
— DIETRICH BONHOEFFER

When the dawn of His gospel broke upon a dark world, Jesus declared: "The time is fulfilled, and the kingdom of God is at hand; repent and believe in the gospel" (Mark 1:15).

In today's language, He might have said, "Reinvent your way of living since the time is ripe for you to step into the irresistible dream of God" (PAR).

Dallas Willard's paraphrase makes Jesus' meaning hard to miss: "All the preliminaries have been taken care of and the rule of God is now accessible to everyone. Review your plans for living and base your life on this remarkable new opportunity."[1]

The apostle Paul, overwhelmed by the vision, in wild, extravagant devotion counted "all things to be loss in view of the surpassing value of knowing Christ Jesus my Lord" (Philippians 3:8).

Ignatius, in the sixteenth century, embraced knowing and loving Christ as his only goal, thereby marginalizing everything else in his life.

At the turn of the twentieth century, the vision of discipleship was stated by Oswald Chambers in these terms: "My goal is God

Himself. . . . At any cost, dear Lord, by any road."[2]

Now, just after the turn of the twenty-first century, here is fresh language for the centuries-old reality: "The vision? The vision is Jesus: obsessively, dangerously, undeniably Jesus."[3]

Different words from different times and places communicating the same reality: Relationship with Jesus is the one thing to be valued above everything. We are invited into this reality because it is the greatest opportunity we will ever have.

A shadow of this reality can be seen in the unprecedented worldwide response to the musical *Les Miserables:*

- Seen by more than 51 million people worldwide
- Box office gross of more than $2 billion
- 38 countries
- 227 cities
- 39,000+ performances
- 23 different languages
- 50 international awards[4]

The drama of redemption taps into the hunger of the human heart at such depths that many are not even conscious of it. The invitation is practically irresistible, but there remains a mystery as to why everyone doesn't respond. They are entertained. They admire. Their hearts may even be moved. Yet they can't bring themselves to let go of their own kingdoms.

The Joyful Cost of Finding Real Life

The kingdom parable of the hidden treasure is jammed with street-level truth about life. One verse, Matthew 13:44, contains the entire parable: "The kingdom of heaven is like a treasure hidden in the field, which a man found and hid again; and from joy over it he goes and sells all that he has and buys that field."

This parable is a great example of earthy, common sense reality. Jesus was not going around spewing surrealistic or idealistic gas. His teaching cuts to the heart and challenges the intellect. The premise is simple and clear: A man happens upon a hidden treasure in a field. In order to get the treasure, he must buy the field. That requires him to sell everything he owns to scrape up enough to purchase the field. He does it with joy. Why? Because this is the deal of a lifetime! Was he worried about what it would cost to buy the field? No, because the treasure was worth far more than the price of the land. He wasn't counting the cost; he was counting his profit.

Jesus says that is what the kingdom of heaven is like. If this were a values clarification exercise, only one choice would be acceptable: Do what you have to do to buy the field with the hidden treasure. In other words, no sacrifice is too great, because the value of what is gained far outweighs what is lost. Do we see that the greatness and goodness of life in the kingdom with Jesus is worth any cost?

Relationships

The so-called "hard saying" of Jesus in Matthew 10:37 should make more sense to you now, after learning from Paul and Ignatius about valuing one thing. Jesus said, "Whoever loves father or mother more than me is not worthy of me; and whoever loves son or daughter more than me is not worthy of me" (NRSV).

Why is this true? Jesus is the hidden treasure of love. If I sell (subjugate) all other relationships for the sake of my relationship with Jesus, then I will be empowered to love in those relationships more deeply than if I had placed them before my relationship with Jesus. By loving Jesus first, I love all others better.

The major part of our earthly "kingdom" is composed of human relationships, so it is vital that we take care not to place them above our love for Christ. Richard Rohr provided the rationale for Jesus' being our first love:

> We cannot welcome the presence, the *parousia*, the full coming of Christ until we've let go of the old. We've lived under the illusion that we could have both: we could idolatrously worship this world order and at the same time say, "Thy Kingdom come." Yet we can't say, "Thy Kingdom come" unless we are willing to say, "My kingdom go."[5]

Possessions

The same dynamic is at work in terms of my material possessions. What initially sounds like a "hard saying" that threatens my security is actually freedom and lasting security. In Luke 12:22-34, Jesus describes the tender care of the heavenly Father for the birds of the air and the flowers of the field and then declares that we, as His children, are far more valuable than ravens and lilies. The reality is that whatever I entrust to an Almighty Father is much safer than what I try to protect and hold on to for myself. Again, the invitation from Jesus is to "seek His kingdom" and let God take care of what I will eat, drink, and wear. In so doing, I no longer have to be fearful or anxious, but I can be "carefree in the care of God" (Luke 12:24, MSG).[6] And I can have the kind of kingdom perspective described by Gregory the Great:

> Therefore let temporal possessions be what you use, eternal things what you desire. Let temporal goods be for use on the way, eternal goods be desired for when you arrive at your goal. Whatever goes on in this world, let it be as it were glanced at from the side. Let the eyes of our minds gaze straight ahead of us, while they are focused intently on the goal to which we shall come.[7]

Success

In Luke 10:17-20, Jesus warns against placing an emphasis on success, even spiritual success—or maybe especially on spiritual success. When I focus on successful results, it quickly becomes about my kingdom. By abandoning outcomes, I put my confidence in Jesus to build His church (see Matthew 16:18), and I am set free to value Jesus more than success. Such was the freedom of Dominique Voillaume:

> All that is not the love of God has no meaning for me. I can truthfully say that I have no interest in anything but the love of God which is in Christ Jesus. If God wants it to, my life will be useful through my word and witness. If He wants it to, my life will bear fruit through my prayers and sacrifices. But the usefulness of my life is His concern, not mine. It would be indecent of me to worry about that.[8]

My Life

Jesus doesn't let up. He goes for the jugular. I have surrendered my relationships, my possessions, and my successes, but in Luke 9:23-24, Jesus goes after what He really wants — you and me: "Then he said to them all, 'If any want to become my followers, let them deny themselves and take up their cross daily and follow me. For those who want to save their life will lose it, and those who lose their life for my sake will save it'" (NRSV).

C. S. Lewis explains Jesus' heart in this way:

> The Christian way is different: harder, and easier. Christ says, "Give me all. I don't want so much of your time and so much of your money and so much of your work: I want

you. I have not come to torment your natural self, but to kill it. No half-measures are any good. . . . I will give you a new self instead. In fact, I will give you Myself: my own will shall become yours."[9]

The only way Jesus can give me His life is if I let go of my life by denying myself and being crucified with Him. But if I continue to want to save *my* life, I will lose both my life and Christ's life.

Andrew Murray described this invitation of Jesus to the life of union:

> If, in our orthodox churches, the abiding in Christ, the living union with Him, the experience of His daily and hourly abiding presence and keeping, were preached with the same distinctness and urgency as His atonement and pardon through His blood, I am confident that many would be found to accept with gladness the invitation to such a life.[10]

We can find examples of those who have responded to Jesus' invitation in some pretty unlikely places. For example, on April 21, 2006, forty-seven-year-old Julio Franco became the oldest player in Major League Baseball history to hit a home run. Just a week later, on the twenty-seventh, he became the oldest player in ninety-seven years to steal a base. With a cloud of skepticism surrounding the sport, Franco's longevity has met suspicion from players and outsiders who doubt that he has stayed in top shape through natural training alone. For example, in 2004 retired outfielder Andy Van Slyke accused Franco of using steroids. Franco's response demonstrated the true source of his remarkable life:

> Tell Andy Van Slyke he's right — I'm on the best juice there

is. I'm juiced up every day, and the name of my juice is Jesus. I'm on his power, his wisdom, his understanding. Andy Van Slyke is right, but the thing he didn't mention was what kind of steroids I'm on. Next time you talk to him, tell him the steroid I'm on is Jesus of Nazareth.[11]

That is not a bad theological statement concerning the life of abiding in Jesus' power, wisdom, and understanding — especially from a baseball player!

Losing What We Can't Keep

In Mark 9:43-47, Jesus teaches that it's better to lose anything in this life than it is to lose the kingdom — better to cripple my body if it makes me whole in spirit; better to throw away my eyesight if by doing so I gain spiritual vision. For what profit is there in gaining the whole world and losing my soul (see Mark 8:36)? Again, Jesus makes value statements in order to invite us to value one thing above all. And, as C. S. Lewis points out, nothing is harder to relinquish than ourselves:

> The terrible thing, the almost impossible thing, is to hand over your whole self — all your wishes and precautions — to Christ. But it is far easier than what we are all trying to do instead. For what we are trying to do is to remain what we call "ourselves," to keep personal happiness as our great aim in life, and yet at the same time be "good."[12]

At the end of the Sermon on the Mount, Jesus teaches that there is only one solid foundation to build a life upon — hearing and acting on the words He taught (see Matthew 6:24). Paul affirms Jesus' teaching when he writes to the Corinthians that Jesus is the only foundation (see 1 Corinthians 3:11). A foundation is what everything else is built upon. There is only one, though there are a number of great houses. My family makes for a great house but a weak foundation. My work is a meaningful house, but if I try to make it the foundation for life, all will come tumbling down. My experience of Jesus is a fantastic house, but even that can't be the foundation — only Jesus and His words.

What we value most automatically becomes the foundation of our lives. It would be wise for every disciple to do a searching spiritual inventory to determine exactly what he or she values most. By doing so, we put ourselves in a position to embrace the foundation we really want instead of drifting onto a foundation by default.

Aron Ralston is a man who was forced in a stark and brutal manner to choose what he valued most. On April 26, 2003, he went off to spend a day hiking, biking, and rappelling in two Utah canyons. As he hiked through a three-foot-wide slot canyon, an 800-pound boulder shifted and pinned his right arm. Two days later, Ralston ran out of water. On Thursday, May 1, after five full days, he realized that he was not going to be rescued and he had a choice to make. What did he value more than anything else? For Ralston, the choice was to do whatever it took to survive. So he amputated his own right hand with a pocketknife — an incredible feat by itself. Then he rappelled sixty feet down to the canyon floor and hiked out to find help.[13]

Ralston's choice, though painful and courageous, was obvious. What good is a right hand on a dead man? He chose life and, in doing so, sacrificed his right hand. But was that a cost or a bargain?

When I say yes to Jesus' invitation to value the one thing above all, I get life — an excess of life, Jesus says (see John 10:10). Without that life from above, of what use are my relationships, my possessions, my successes, my own life? Jesus put it as plainly as possible: "What does it profit a man to gain the whole world, and forfeit his soul?" (Mark 8:36).

Ambrose, the Bishop of Milan in the fourth century, provides our conclusion by directing our focus on Jesus, the highest value, and relationship to Him, which is the one true thing:

> God's word is uttered by those who repeat Christ's teaching and meditate on his sayings. Let us always speak this word. When we speak about wisdom, we are speaking of Christ. When we speak about virtue, we are speaking of Christ. When we speak about justice, we are speaking of Christ. When we speak about peace, we are speaking of Christ. When we speak about truth and life and redemption, we are speaking of Christ.[14]

Afterword

As St. Ambrose has written: "Jesus is all things to us if we will."
Therefore I will have nothing else but him; and I have all if I have him.
— MARK FRANK

S o what will be the effects of seeking, choosing, and valuing the
one thing? Isaiah the prophet paints a vivid picture:

Is not this the fast that I choose:
　　to loose the bonds of injustice,
　　to undo the thongs of the yoke,
to let the oppressed go free,
　　and to break every yoke?
Is it not to share your bread with the hungry,
　　and bring the homeless poor into your house;
when you see the naked, to cover them,
　　and not to hide yourself from your own kin?
Then your light shall break forth like the dawn,
　　and your healing shall spring up quickly;
your vindicator shall go before you,
　　the glory of the LORD shall be your rear guard.
Then you shall call, and the LORD will answer;
　　you shall cry for help, and he will say, Here I am.

If you remove the yoke from among you,
　　the pointing of the finger, the speaking of evil,

if you offer your food to the hungry
    and satisfy the needs of the afflicted,
then your light shall rise in the darkness
    and your gloom be like the noonday.
The LORD will guide you continually,
    and satisfy your needs in parched places,
    and make your bones strong;
and you shall be like a watered garden,
    like a spring of water,
    whose waters never fail.
Your ancient ruins shall be rebuilt;
    you shall raise up the foundations of many generations;
you shall be called the repairer of the breach,
    the restorer of streets to live in.
        (Isaiah 58:6-12, NRSV)

In closing, let me suggest a few others:

- *Toward God* — "God will be our love and our longing, God will be all we want and all we strive for, all we think about, all we talk about, our very breath."[1]
- *Toward Jesus* — "We will never understand the full meaning of Jesus' richly varied ministry unless we see how the many things are rooted in the one thing: listening to the Father in the intimacy of perfect love."[2]
- *Toward others*— "Let us visit Christ whenever we may; let us care for him, feed him, clothe him, welcome him, honour him. . . . Let us then show him mercy in the persons of the poor and those who today are lying on the ground, so that when we come to leave this world, they in turn may receive us into everlasting dwelling places, in Christ our Lord himself to whom be glory for ever and ever.[3]

■ *Toward ourselves* —

'Twas battered and scarred, and the auctioneer
Thought it scarcely worth his while
To waste much time on the old violin,
But he held it up with a smile;
"What am I bidden, good folks," he cried
"Who'll start the bidding for me?"
"A dollar, a dollar, now two, only two
Two dollars, and who'll make it three?
Three dollars once, three dollars twice
Going for three." But no —
From the room far back, a gray haired man
Came forward and picked up the bow.
Then wiping the dust from the old violin
And tightening up all the strings
He played a melody pure and sweet,
As sweet as the angel sings.
The music ceased and the auctioneer
With a voice that was quiet and low
Said, "What am I bid for the old violin?"
And he held it up with the bow.
"A thousand dollars, and who'll make it two?
Two thousand and who'll make it three?
Three thousand once, three thousand twice
And going, and gone," said he.
The people cheered, but some of them cried,
"We do not quite understand —
What changed its worth?" Swift came the reply,
"The touch of the master's hand."
And many a man with life out of tune,

And battered and torn with sin
Is auctioned cheap to a thoughtless crowd,
Much like the old violin.
A mess of pottage, a life of shame,
A game and he travels on.
He's going once, and going twice,
He's going and almost gone.
But the Master comes and the foolish crowd
Never can quite understand
The worth of a soul and the change that's wrought
By the touch of the Master's hand.[4]

Jesus is "the Alpha and the Omega, the first and the last, the beginning and the end" (Revelation 22:13). So our New Testament opens with "The record of the genealogy of Jesus the Messiah" (Matthew 1:1) and closes with "Come, Lord Jesus. The grace of the Lord Jesus be with all. Amen" (Revelation 22:20-21).

Notes

Preface

1. Donald Miller, "Don Miller Isn't Hip: A Gospel for People Tired of Trying to Be Cool," interview by *Leadership Journal* editors, *Out of Ur*, May 15, 2006, http://blog.christianitytoday.com/ outofur/archives/2006/05/donald_miller_i.html.
2. Francis de Sales, *Introduction to the Devout Life* (New York: Vintage Books, 2002), xl.

Introduction: The Only True Thing

1. Commonly known as the Great Commission. See Matthew 28:19–20.
2. Commonly known as the Great Commandment. See Matthew 22:36–40.
3. This phrase comes from A. W. Tozer's mountain of a book, *The Pursuit of God* (Camp Hill, PA: Christian Publications, 1982). Please, if you have not read it, put this book down and go read Tozer.
4. John Calvin, *The Institutes of Christian Religion* (Grand Rapids, MI: Christian Classics Ethereal Library), bk. 1, chap. 5, http:// www.ccel.org/ccel/calvin/institutes.iv.i.vi.html.
5. Tozer, 19.
6. Francis de Sales, *Introduction to the Devout Life* (New York: Vintage Books, 2002), 7.

7. Douglas Steere, introduction to *Purity of Heart Is to Will One Thing*, by Søren Kierkegaard, trans. Douglas Steere (New York: Harper and Row, 1956), 23.

8. Oswald Chambers, *My Utmost for His Highest* (Burlington, Ontario: Welch Publishing, 1963), 103.

9. The latest in the long line of celebrities, millionaires, rock stars, and athletes who have voiced this cry is Tom Brady. In a November 6, 2005, edition of the CBS news program *60 Minutes*, Brady, who at the age of twenty-eight has won three Super Bowls as a quarterback for the New England Patriots; is financially set for life with a multimillion-dollar, long-term contract; has a family that loves and supports him; dates an actress; and has millions of fans, was asked, "What's next for you?" His response was, "I don't know, but there has to be more." Of course, he is right — there is more. But will he be another rich young ruler who has it all but goes away grieving (see Matthew 19:22)?

10. Chambers, 6.

11. C. S. Lewis, *Mere Christianity* (New York: Macmillan, 1952), 56.

Part 1: Seeking the One Thing — A Pure and Holy Passion

Chapter 1: Psalm 27

1. A. W. Tozer, *Signposts: A Collection of Sayings by A. W. Tozer*, ed. Harry Verploegh (Wheaton, IL: Victor, 1988), 58.

2. John Calvin, *Heart Aflame: Daily Readings from Calvin on the Psalms* (Philipsburg, NJ: P & R, 1999), 95.

3. *The Renovare Spiritual Formation Bible* (San Francisco: HarperSanFrancisco, 2005) does a beautiful job of demonstrating book by book that the with-God life is the primary theme of the Scriptures.

4. C. S. Lewis, *The Weight of Glory*, rev. ed. (New York: Macmillan, 1980), 16.

5. For Peter's own picture of what this process entails, read 2 Peter 1.

6. Galatians 4:19 and Romans 8:29 supply the vocabulary for what has become known as "spiritual formation."

7. See Psalms 11:4; 18:6; 29:9.

8. Artur Weiser, *The Psalms: A Commentary*, trans. Herbert Hartwell (Philadelphia: Westminster, 1962), 247.

9. "The Prayer of the Unknown Confederate Soldier," quoted in *Moments of Transcendence*, ed. Rabbi Dov Peretz Elkins (Northvale, NJ: Jason Aronson, 1994), 144.

Chapter 2: Julian of Norwich

1. A woman who made solemn vows to be attached, or "anchored," to a particular church for a semi-reclusive life of prayer, study, intercession, and spiritual guidance.

2. James L. Snyder, *In Pursuit of God: The Life of A.W. Tozer* (Camp Hill, PA: Christian Publications, 1991), 156.

3. Kelby Cotton, "Julian of Norwich," *Higher Ground*, 1997, http://www.lifeofprayer.org/growth/hg/julian1a.htm.

4. Anne Savage and Nicholas Watson, trans., *Anchoritic Spirituality: Ancrene Wisse and Associated Works* (Mahwah, NJ: Paulist, 1987), 15–16.

5. Savage and Watson, 16.

6. Savage and Watson, 18.

7. Savage and Watson, 18.

8. Savage and Watson, 18.

9. Savage and Watson, 22.

10. Savage and Watson, 24.

11. Julian of Norwich, *Julian of Norwich: Showings*, trans. Edmund College and James Walsh (Mahwah, NJ: Paulist, 1978), 342.

12. Julian of Norwich, 179.

13. Julian of Norwich, 256–257.

14. Julian of Norwich, 179.

15. Julian of Norwich, 191.

16. Julian of Norwich, 315.

17. Julian of Norwich, 161.

18. Julian of Norwich, 340.

19. Julian of Norwich, 328.

20. Julian of Norwich, 149.

21. Julian of Norwich, 267.

22. Julian of Norwich, 320.

23. Julian of Norwich, 321.

24. Many excellent resources are available for the discovery of helpful spiritual practices. In my earlier book, *Soul Keeping* (Colorado Springs, CO: NavPress, 1998), I devoted a chapter each to praying the psalms, silence and solitude, meditative prayer, spiritual direction, receiving grace, and practicing humility. A more complete treatment of spiritual disciplines can be found in Richard Foster's classic *The Celebration of Discipline* (San Francisco: HarperSanFrancisco, 1998) and in Dallas Willard's *The Spirit of the Disciplines* (New York: HarperCollins, 1988). Recent contributions include Tony Jones's *The Sacred Way* (Grand Rapids, MI: Zondervan, 2005) and Adele Calhoun's *Spiritual Disciplines Handbook* (Downers Grove, IL: InterVarsity, 2005).

25. Julian of Norwich, 244–245.

26. Columbanus, quoted in Robert Atwell, ed., *Celebrating the Seasons: Daily Spiritual Readings for the Christian Year* (Harrisburg, PA: Morehouse, 2001), 13.

Chapter 3: Jesus' Invitation to Seek the One Thing

1. Though often ascribed to Chesterton, according to the American Chesterton Society website, "we have discovered that the only documented source of this quotation is the book *The World, The Flesh, and Father Smith* by Bruce Marshall ([Houghton Mifflin,] 1945). And the quote is really: '. . . the young man who rings the bell at the brothel is unconsciously looking for God.' (p. 108)." http://www.chesterton.org/qmeister2/qmeister.htm.

2. A. W. Tozer, *Signposts: A Collection of Sayings from A. W. Tozer*, ed. Harry Verploegh (Wheaton, IL: Victor, 1988), 57.

3. To learn more about first-century Palestinian Judaism, see Ray Vander Laan's *Echoes of His Presence* (Grand Rapids, MI: Zondervan, 1996), from which I gathered some of these facts.

4. Gertrude the Great, quoted in Hugh Feiss, *Monastic Wisdom: Writings on the Contemplative Life* (San Francisco: HarperSanFrancisco, 1999), 180.

5. C. S. Lewis, *The Weight of Glory* (Grand Rapids, MI: Eerdmans, 1965), 2.

6. Henri Nouwen, *One Necessary Thing*, ed. Wendy Wilson Greer (New York: Crossroad, 1999), 31.

7. Nouwen, 28.

8. George MacDonald, quoted at http://en.thinkexist.com/quotes/george_macdonald.

9. Evelyn Underhill, quoted in *Disciplines for the Inner Life*, ed. Bob Benson and Michael W. Benson (Waco, TX: Word, 1985), 194.

10. Oswald Chambers, *My Utmost for His Highest* (Burlington, Ontario: Welch, 1963), 85.

11. C. S. Lewis, quoted in Randy Alcorn, *Money, Possessions, and Eternity* (Wheaton, IL: Tyndale, 2003), 15.

12. Columbanus, quoted in Robert Atwell, ed., *Celebrating the Seasons: Daily Spiritual Readings for the Christian Year* (Harrisburg, PA: Morehouse, 2001), 20.

13. A. W. Tozer, *The Pursuit of God* (Camp Hill, PA: Christian Publications, 1993), 11–12.

14. Jean-Pierre de Caussade, quoted in Atwell, 494.

15. Walter Liefeld and Linda Cannell, "Spiritual Formation and Theological Education," in *Alive to God: Studies in Spirituality*, ed. J. I. Packer and Loren Wilkinson (Downers Grove, IL: InterVarsity, 1992), 239.

16. Anselm, quoted in Frederick J. Schumacher and Dorothy A. Zelenko, eds., *For All the Saints: A Prayer Book for and by the Church* (Delhi, NY: American Lutheran Publicity Bureau, 1996), 4:252.

Part 2: Choosing the One Thing — A Magnificent Obsession

Chapter 4: Luke 10:38-42

1. William Law, *A Serious Call to a Devout and Holy Life* (Grand Rapids, MI: Christian Classics Ethereal Library, 2000), http://www.ccel.org/ccel/law/serious_call.ii.html.

2. Oswald Chambers, *Devotions for a Deeper Life* (Grand Rapids, MI: Zondervan, 1986), 20.

3. Along with the current passage, see also John 11:32 and 12:3.

4. *M. 'Abot* 1:4, cited by Darrell L. Bock, *Luke: 9:51–24:53* (Grand Rapids, MI: Baker, 1996), 1040.

5. A. Oepke, *Theological Dictionary of the New Testament*, eds. Gerhard Kittel and Gerhard Friedrich, and trans. Geoffrey Bromiley (Grand Rapids, MI: Eerdmans, 1964), 1:781–782.

6. In the Greek, the grammar demonstrates that she *decided* to seat herself beside Jesus. The Greek verb is an aorist passive participle used in the reflexive sense of "having seated herself

beside." See *The Anchor Bible: The Gospel According to Luke X– XXIV: A New Translation with Introduction and Commentary by Joseph Fitzmeyer* (New York: Doubleday, 1985), 893.

7. Jonathan Edwards, quoted in Frederick J. Schumacher and Dorothy A. Zelenko, eds., *For All the Saints: A Prayer Book for and by the Church* (Delhi, NY: American Lutheran Publicity Bureau, 1994), 1:56.

8. Tito Colliander, *Way of the Ascetics* (Crestwood, NY: St. Vladimir's Seminary Press, 1988), vii.

9. See Luke 8:18; 12:19-21, and 12:33 for some pretty amazing promises.

10. Jean Pierre de Caussade, *The Sacrament of the Present Moment* (San Francisco: HarperSanFrancisco, 1989), 9.

11. A. W. Tozer, *The Pursuit of God* (Camp Hill, PA: Christian Publications, 1993), 96.

12. Oswald Chambers, *My Utmost for His Highest* (Burlington, Ontario: Welch, 1963), 72.

13. Henri Nouwen, *Jesus: A Gospel* (Maryknoll, NY: Orbis, 2001), 142.

Chapter 5: Søren Kierkegaard

1. Douglas Steere, introduction to *Purity of Heart Is to Will One Thing*, by Søren Kierkegaard, trans. Douglas Steere (New York: Harper and Row, 1956), 13.

2. Alexander Dru, ed., *The Journals of Søren Kierkegaard* (London: Oxford University Press, 1938), 773.

3. Dru, 748.

4. Dru, 125.

5. *USA Today*, "450 Sheep Jump to Their Deaths in Turkey," July 8, 2005, http://www.usatoday.com/news/offbeat/2005-07-08 -sheep-suicide_x.htm?csp=34.

6. Steere, 16.
7. Dru, 16.
8. Søren Kierkegaard, *Training in Chrisitanity*, trans. Walter Lowrie (Princeton: Princeton University Press, 1944), 151.
9. Perry LeFevre, ed., *The Prayers of Kierkegaard* (Chicago: University of Chicago Press, 1956), 208.
10. Kierkegaard, *Training*, 227.
11. LeFevre, 205.
12. Dru, 1262.
13. LeFevre, 220.
14. Dru, 22.
15. LeFevre, 203.
16. Søren Kierkegaard, *Edifying Discourses*, trans. David F. Swenson and Lillian Marvin Swenson (Minneapolis: Augsburg, 1946), 142.
17. LeFevre, 203.
18. Dru, 754.
19. Dru, 754.
20. LeFevre, 202.
21. Søren Kierkegaard, *Christian Discourses*, trans. Walter Lowrie (London: Oxford University Press, 1940), 323.
22. Kierkegaard, *Purity*, 218.

Chapter 6: Jesus' Invitation to Choose the One Thing

1. C. S. Lewis, *The Silver Chair* (New York: Macmillan, 1953), 17.
2. George MacDonald, *Diary of an Old Soul* (Minneapolis: Augsburg, 1975), 54.
3. Dallas Willard, *The Divine Conspiracy* (San Francisco: HarperSanFrancisco, 1998), 297. I recommend spending at least a year reading, studying, and meditating on this book.
4. For a lively discussion of rabbis and their "yokes," see Rob Bell's fascinating and powerful book, *Velvet Elvis* (Grand Rapids, MI:

Zondervan, 2005), especially chapters 2, 4, and 5.

5. Dallas Willard, *The Spirit of the Disciplines* (San Francisco: Harper and Row, 1988), 252.

6. Francis de Sales, *Introduction to the Devout Life* (New York: Vintage Spiritual Classics, 2002), 7.

7. Andre Louf, quoted in Richard Foster and Emilie Griffin, eds., *Spiritual Classics* (San Francisco: HarperSanFrancisco, 2000), 33.

8. For an excellent resource on this topic, see Brother Lawrence's book *The Practice of the Presence of God*. I highly recommend the edition translated by John Delaney (New York: Doubleday, 1977).

9. John Henry Newman, quoted in Frederick J. Schumacher and Dorothy A. Zelenko, eds., *For All the Saints: A Prayer Book for and by the Church* (Delhi, NY: American Lutheran Publicity Bureau, 1994), 1:871.

Part 3: Valuing the One Thing — A Glorious Ambition

Chapter 7: Philippians 3

1. Colin Brown, ed., *The New International Dictionary of New Testament Theology* (Grand Rapids, MI: Zondervan, 1986), 480.

2. David Livingstone, quoted in Frederick J. Schumacher and Dorothy A. Zelenko, eds., *For All the Saints: A Prayer Book for and by the Church* (Delhi, NY: American Lutheran Publicity Bureau, 1995), 3:244.

3. Dallas Willard, *The Divine Conspiracy* (San Francisco: HarperSanFrancisco, 1998), 55.

4. Jonathan Edwards, quoted in Richard Foster and James Bryan Smith, eds., *Devotional Classics* (San Francisco: HarperSanFrancisco, 1993), 21.

5. Ignatius of Antioch, *Apostolic Fathers I, The Letter to the Trallians*, trans. Kirsopp Lake (London: Loeb, 1912), 222.
6. Philip Jacob Spener, quoted in Schumacher and Zelenko, 1:782.
7. Oswald Chambers, *My Utmost for His Highest* (Burlington, Ontario: Welch, 1963), 204–205.
8. John Oxenham, quoted in Schumacher and Zelenko, 4:1067.
9. Augustine, quoted in Schumacher and Zelenko, 3:927.

Chapter 8: Ignatius of Loyola

1. Michael G. Harter, ed., *Hearts on Fire: Praying with the Jesuits* (St. Louis: Institute of Jesuit Sources, 1993), 7.
2. George Ganss, ed., *Ignatius of Loyola: Spiritual Exercises and Selected Works* (New York: Paulist, 1991), 15.
3. David L. Fleming, *The Spiritual Exercises of St. Ignatius: A Literal Translation and a Contemporary Reading* (St. Louis: The Institute of Jesuit Resources, 1978), 6.
4. By most accounts, *The Imitation of Christ* is the most read book in Christian history apart from the Bible. The translation by William Creasy (Notre Dame, IN: Ave Maria Press, 1989) is the best modern rendition. For a paraphrased translation similar to Eugene Peterson's translation of the Bible, *The Message* (Colorado Springs, CO: NavPress, 2002), pick up William Griffin's earthy and humorous version (New York: HarperCollins, 2000).
5. Ganss, 45.
6. Fleming, 21 (emphasis added).
7. Fleming, 23.
8. Fleming, 23.
9. Fleming, 23.
10. Fleming, 23.
11. Fleming, 23.
12. Fleming, 23.

13. Eugene Peterson, *Eat This Book: A Conversation in the Art of Spiritual Reading* (Grand Rapids, MI: Eerdmans, 2006), 17.
14. C. S. Lewis, *An Experiment in Criticism* (Cambridge: Cambridge University Press, 1961), 88.
15. Thomas Kelly, *A Testament of Devotion* (New York: Harper and Row, 1941), 122.

Chapter 9: Jesus' Invitation to Value the One Thing

1. Dallas Willard, *The Divine Conspiracy* (San Francisco: HarperSanFrancisco, 1998), 15.
2. Oswald Chambers, *My Utmost for His Highest* (Burlington, Ontario: Welch, 1963), 239.
3. Pete Greig, *The Vision and the Vow* (Lake Mary, FL: Relevant Books, 2004), no page number. I love this book and the movement it represents. Get it, read it, be a part of it. Check out the website, www.mustardseedorder.com.
4. John Moore, "18 Years on Tour and 'Les Mis' Still Stirs," *The Denver Post*, May 1, 2006.
5. Richard Rohr with John Bookser Feister, *Jesus' Plan for a New World: The Sermon on the Mount* (Cincinnati: St. Anthony Messenger Press, 1996), 33.
6. I would encourage you to read this entire passage in *The Message*. Powerful!
7. Gregory the Great, quoted in Frederick J. Schumacher and Dorothy A. Zelenko, eds., *For All the Saints: A Prayer Book for and by the Church* (Delhi, NY: American Lutheran Publicity Bureau, 1995), 3:1213.
8. Dominique Voillaume, quoted in Brennan Manning, *Signature of Jesus* (Old Tappan, NJ: Chosen Books, 1988), 77.
9. C. S. Lewis, *Mere Christianity* (San Francisco: HarperSanFrancisco, 2001), 196–197.

10. Andrew Murray, quoted in Schumacher and Zelenko, 3:1091–1092.

11. Quoted in *Preaching Today*, http://www.preachingtoday .com/34982.

12. Lewis, 197–198.

13. Joanne Kelley, "Arm Loss Prelude to New Life," *Rocky Mountain News*, July 15, 2006.

14. Ambrose, quoted in Robert Atwell, ed., *Celebrating the Seasons: Daily Spiritual Readings for the Christian Year* (Harrisburg, PA: Morehouse, 2001), 339.

Afterword

1. John Cassian, *Conferences*, trans. Colm Lubheid (Mahwah, NJ: Paulist, 1985), 7.

2. Henri Nouwen, *Jesus: A Gospel* (Maryknoll, NY: Orbis, 2001), 139.

3. Gregory of Nazianzus, quoted in Robert Atwell, ed., *Celebrating the Seasons: Daily Spiritual Readings for the Christian Year* (Harrisburg, PA: Morehouse, 2001), 181.

4. Anonymous, "The Touch of the Master's Hand," quoted in Frederick J. Schumacher and Dorothy A. Zelenko, eds., *For All the Saints: A Prayer Book for and by the Church* (Delhi, NY: American Lutheran Publicity Bureau, 1995), 3:892–894.

About the Author

MR. HOWARD BAKER serves on the full-time faculty of Denver Seminary as Instructor of Christian Formation and as Campus Chaplain. He joined Denver Seminary as adjunct instructor in 1995 and has taught in the areas of spiritual formation and spiritual direction. In 1999, together with Dr. Bruce Demarest, he began the Seminary's certificate program in Evangelical Spiritual Guidance. He continues to teach in the current certificate program in Christian Formation and Soul Care. In addition, he serves with the Spiritual Formation Alliance, offers spiritual direction, leads retreats, and is on the board of Young Life Africa.

He earned a Bachelor of Arts degree from Texas Christian University, a Master of Theology degree from Dallas Theological Seminary, and a Certificate in Spiritual Direction from St. Thomas Seminary. He is currently working toward a PhD in Theology from Trinity College, University of Bristol.

Prior to coming to Denver Seminary, Mr. Baker served Young Life, a mission to adolescents, as an Area and Regional Director, was a chaplain at the Denver Rescue Mission, and co-taught the Vincentian Formation Program for Spiritual Directors. He also teaches at Fuller Seminary, Colorado, and has taught as a visiting faculty member at St. Meinrad Seminary, Summit Bible College, Colorado Christian University, and Evangelical Theological College (Ethiopia).

He authored *Soul Keeping*, contributed to *The Transformation of a Man's Heart* and to the *Renovare Spiritual Formation Bible*, and was consulting editor for *Between Heaven and Earth: Prayers and Reflections That Celebrate an Intimate God.* He has written articles for *Christianity, Discipleship Journal,* and *Kindred Spirit.*

SATISFY YOUR NEED FOR CONTENTMENT.

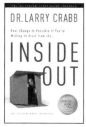

.